The Mousetrap

A Play

by Agatha Christie

A SAMUEL FRENCH ACTING EDITION

SAMUEL FRENCH

FOUNDED 1830

New York Hollywood London Toronto

SAMUELFRENCH.COM

THE MOUSETRAP

Presented by Peter Saunders at the Ambassadors Theatre, London, W.C.2, on 25th November 1952 with the following cast of characters:

(in the order of their appearance)

MOLLIE RALSTON	*Sheila Sim*
GILES RALSTON	*John Paul*
CHRISTOPHER WREN	*Allan McClelland*
MRS BOYLE	*Mignon O'Doherty*
MAJOR METCALF	*Aubrey Dexter*
MISS CASEWELL	*Jessica Spencer*
MR PARAVICINI	*Martin Miller*
DETECTIVE SERGEANT TROTTER	*Richard Attenborough*

The play produced by Peter Cotes

Décor by Roger Furse

SYNOPSIS OF SCENES

ACT I

SCENE 1   The Great Hall at Monkswell Manor.   Late afternoon
SCENE 2   The same. The following day after lunch

ACT II

The same. Ten minutes later

Time: *the present*

THE MOUSETRAP

ACT I

Scene 1

Scene—*The Great Hall at Monkswell Manor. Late afternoon.*

The house looks not so much a period piece but a house which has been lived in by generations of the same family with dwindling resources. There are tall windows up C; a big arched opening up R leading to the entrance hall, the front door and the kitchen; and an arched opening L leading upstairs to the bedrooms. Up L leading off the stairs is the door to the library; down L is the door to the drawing-room; and down R the door (opening on stage) to the dining-room. R is an open fireplace and beneath the window up C a window seat and a radiator.

The Hall is furnished as a lounge. There is some good old oak, including a large refectory table by the window up C, an oak chest in the entrance hall up R, and a stool on the stairs L. The curtains and the upholstered furniture—a sofa LC, an armchair C, a large leather armchair R, and a small Victorian armchair down R—are shabby and old-fashioned. There is a combined desk and bookcase L, with a radio and telephone on it and a chair beside it. There is another chair up RC by the window, a Canterbury containing newspapers and magazines above the fireplace and a small half circular card table behind the sofa. There are two wall brackets over the fireplace which are worked together; and a wall bracket on the L wall, one L of the library door and one in the entrance hall, which are also worked together. There are double switches L of the arch up R, and on the downstage side of the door down L, and a single switch on the upstage side of the door down R. A table lamp stands on the sofa table.

(See the Photograph of the scene and the Ground Plan)

Before the CURTAIN *rises the House Lights fade to a complete* BLACK-OUT *and the music of "Three Blind Mice" is heard.*

When the CURTAIN *rises the stage is in complete darkness. The music fades giving place to a shrill whistle of the same tune, "Three Blind Mice". A woman's piercing scream is heard then a mixture of male and female voices saying: "My God, what's that?" "Went that way!" "Oh, my God!" Then a police whistle sounds, followed by several other police whistles, all of which fade to silence.*

VOICE ON THE RADIO. . . . and according to Scotland Yard, the crime took place at twenty-four Culver Street, Paddington.

The LIGHTS *come up, revealing the Hall at Monkswell Manor. It is late afternoon, and almost dark. Snow can be seen falling heavily through the windows up c. There is a fire burning. A freshly-painted sign board is standing on its side on the stairs against the archway L; it has on it in large letters:* MONKWELL MANOR GUEST HOUSE.

The murdered woman was a Mrs Maureen Lyon. In connexion with the murder, the police are anxious to interview a man seen in the vicinity, wearing a dark overcoat, light scarf, and a soft felt hat.

(MOLLIE RALSTON *enters through the arch up* R. *She is a tall, pretty young woman with an ingenuous air, in her twenties. She puts down her handbag and gloves on the armchair* C *then crosses to the radio and switches it off during the next speech. She places a small parcel in the desk cupboard*)

Motorists are warned against ice-bound roads. The heavy snow is expected to continue, and throughout the country there will be a certain freezing, particularly at points on the north and north-east coast of Scotland.

MOLLIE (*calling*) Mrs Barlow! Mrs Barlow! (*Receiving no reply she crosses to the armchair* C, *picks up her handbag and one glove and then goes out through the arch up* R. *She removes her overcoat and then returns*) Brr! It's cold. (*She goes to the wall switch above the door down* R *and switches on the wall brackets over the fireplace. She moves up to the window, feels the radiator and draws the curtains. Then she moves down to the sofa table and switches on the table lamp. She looks round and notices the large sign board lying on its side on the stairs. She picks it up and places it against the wall* L *of the window alcove. She steps back, nodding her head*) It really does look nice—oh! (*She notices that there is no "S" on the sign*) How stupid of Giles. (*She looks at her watch then at the clock*) Gosh!

(MOLLIE *hurries off up the stairs* L.

GILES *enters from the front door* R. *He is a rather arrogant but attractive young man in his twenties. He stamps his feet to shake off the snow, opens the oak chest and puts inside a big paper carrier he has been carrying. He takes off his overcoat, hat and scarf, moves down and throws them on the armchair* C. *Then he goes to the fire and warms his hands*)

GILES (*calling*) Mollie? Mollie? Mollie? Where are you?

(MOLLIE *enters from the arch* L)

MOLLIE (*cheerfully*) Doing all the work, you brute. (*She crosses to Giles*)

GILES. Oh, there you are—leave it all to me. Shall I stoke the Aga?

MOLLIE. Done.

GILES (*kissing her*) Hullo, sweetheart. Your nose is cold.

MOLLIE. I've just come in. (*She crosses to the fire*)

GILES. Why? Where have you been? Surely you've not been out in this weather?

MOLLIE. I had to go down to the village for some stuff I'd forgotten. Did you get the chicken netting?

GILES. It wasn't the right kind. (*He sits on the left arm of the armchair* C) I went on to another dump but that wasn't any good either. Practically a whole day wasted. My God, I'm half frozen. Car was skidding like anything. The snow's coming down thick. What do you bet we're not snowed up tomorrow?

MOLLIE. Oh dear, I do hope not. (*She crosses to the radiator and feels it*) If only the pipes don't freeze.

GILES (*rising and moving up to Mollie*) We'll have to keep the central heating well stoked up. (*He feels the radiator*) H'm, not too good—I wish they'd send the coke along. We've not got any too much.

MOLLIE (*moving down to the sofa and sitting*) Oh! I do so want everything to go well at first. First impressions are so important.

GILES (*moving down to* R *of the sofa*) Is everything ready? Nobody's arrived yet, I suppose?

MOLLIE. No, thank goodness. I think everything's in order. Mrs Barlow's hooked it early. Afraid of the weather, I suppose.

GILES. What a nuisance these daily women are. That leaves everything on your shoulders.

MOLLIE. *And* yours! This is a partnership.

GILES (*crossing to the fire*) So long as you don't ask me to cook.

MOLLIE (*rising*) No, no, that's my department. Anyway, we've got lots of tins in case we are snowed up. (*Crossing to Giles*) Oh, Giles, do you think it's going to be all right?

GILES. Got cold feet, have you? Are you sorry now we didn't sell the place when your aunt left it to you, instead of having this mad idea of running it as a guest house?

MOLLIE. No, I'm not. I love it. And talking of a guest house. Just look at *that*! (*She indicates the sign board in an accusing manner*)

GILES (*complacently*) Pretty good, what? (*He crosses to* L *of the sign board*)

MOLLIE. It's a disaster! Don't you see? You've left out the "S". Monkwell instead of Monkswell.

GILES. Good Lord, so I did. However did I come to do that? But it doesn't really matter, does it? Monkwell is just as good a name.

MOLLIE. You're in disgrace. (*She crosses to the desk*) Go and stoke up the central heating.

GILES. Across that icy yard! Ugh! Shall I bank it up for the night now?

MOLLIE. No, you don't do that until ten or eleven o'clock at night.

GILES. How appalling!

MOLLIE. Hurry up. Someone may arrive at any minute now.

GILES. You've got all the rooms worked out?

MOLLIE. Yes. (*She sits at the desk and picks up a paper from it*) Mrs Boyle, Front Fourposter Room. Major Metcalf, Blue Room. Miss Casewell, East Room. Mr Wren, Oak Room.

GILES (*crossing to R of the sofa table*) I wonder what all these people will be like. Oughtn't we to have got rent in advance?

MOLLIE. Oh no, I don't think so.

GILES. We're rather mugs at this game.

MOLLIE. They bring luggage. If they don't pay we hang on to their luggage. It's quite simple.

GILES. I can't help thinking we ought to have taken a correspondence course in hotel keeping. We're sure to get had in some way. Their luggage might be just bricks wrapped up in newspaper and where should we be then?

MOLLIE. They all wrote from very good addresses.

GILES. That's what servants with forged references do. Some of these people may be criminals hiding from the police. (*He moves up to the sign board and picks it up*)

MOLLIE. I don't care what they are so long as they pay us seven guineas every week.

GILES. You're such a wonderful woman of business, Mollie.

(GILES *exits through the arch up* R, *carrying the sign board.* MOLLIE *switches on the radio*)

VOICE ON THE RADIO. And according to Scotland Yard, the crime took place at twenty-four Culver Street, Paddington. The murdered woman was a Mrs Maureen Lyon. In connexion with the murder, the police——

(MOLLIE *rises and crosses to the armchair* C)

—are anxious to interview a man seen in the vicinity, wearing a dark overcoat——

(MOLLIE *picks up Giles' overcoat*)

—light scarf——

(MOLLIE *picks up his scarf*)

—and a soft felt hat.

(MOLLIE *picks up his hat and exits through the arch up* R)

Motorists are warned against ice-bound roads.

(*The door bell rings*)

The heavy snow is expected to continue, and throughout the country . . .

(MOLLIE *enters, crosses to the desk, switches off the radio and hurries off through the arch up* R)

MOLLIE (*off*) How do you do?
CHRISTOPHER (*off*) Thanks so much.

(CHRISTOPHER WREN *enters through the arch up* R *with a suitcase which he places* R *of the refectory table. He is a rather wild-looking neurotic young man. His hair is long and untidy and he wears a woven artistic tie. He has a confiding, almost childish manner.*
MOLLIE *enters and moves up* C)

Weather is simply awful. My taxi gave up at your gate. (*He crosses and places his hat on the sofa table*) Wouldn't attempt the drive. No sporting instinct. (*Moving up to Mollie*) Are you Mrs Ralston? How delightful! My name's Wren.
MOLLIE. How do you do, Mr Wren?
CHRISTOPHER. You know you're not at all as I'd pictured you. I've been thinking of you as a retired General's widow, Indian Army. I thought you'd be terrifically grim and Memsahibish, and that the whole place would be simply crammed with Benares brass. Instead, it's heavenly (*crossing below the sofa to* L *of the sofa table*)—quite heavenly. Lovely proportions. (*Pointing at the desk*) That's a fake! (*Pointing at the sofa table*) Ah, but this table's genuine. I'm simply going to love this place. (*He moves below the armchair* C) Have you got any wax flowers or birds of Paradise?
MOLLIE. I'm afraid not.
CHRISTOPHER. What a pity! Well, what about a sideboard? A purple plummy mahogany sideboard with great solid carved fruits on it?
MOLLIE. Yes, we have—in the dining-room. (*She glances at the door down* R)
CHRISTOPHER (*following her glance*) In here? (*He moves down* R *and opens the door*) I must see it.

(CHRISTOPHER *exits into the dining-room and* MOLLIE *follows him.*
GILES *enters through the archway up* R. *He looks round and examines the suitcase.*
Hearing voices from the dining-room, GILES *exits up* R)

MOLLIE (*off*) Do come and warm yourself.

(MOLLIE *enters from the dining-room, followed by* CHRISTOPHER. MOLLIE *moves* C)

CHRISTOPHER (*as he enters*) Absolutely perfect. Real bedrock respectability. But why do away with a centre mahogany table? (*Looking off* R) Little tables just spoil the effect.

(GILES *enters up* R *and stands* L *of the large armchair* R)

MOLLIE. We thought guests would prefer them—this is my husband.

CHRISTOPHER (*moving up to Giles and shaking hands with him*) How do you do? Terrible weather, isn't it? Takes one back to Dickens and Scrooge and that irritating Tiny Tim. So bogus. (*He turns towards the fire*) Of course, Mrs Ralston, you're absolutely right about the little tables. I was being carried away by my feeling for period. If you had a mahogany dining-table, you'd have to have the right family round it. (*He turns to Giles*) Stern handsome father with a beard, prolific, faded mother, eleven children of assorted ages, a grim governess, and somebody called "poor Harriet", the poor relation who acts as general dogsbody and is very, *very* grateful for being given a good home!

GILES (*disliking him*) I'll take your suitcase upstairs for you. (*He picks up the suitcase. To Mollie*) Oak Room, did you say?

MOLLIE. Yes.

CHRISTOPHER. I do hope that it's got a fourposter with little chintz roses?

GILES. It hasn't.

(GILES *exits* L *up the stairs with the suitcase*)

CHRISTOPHER. I don't believe your husband is going to like me. (*Moving a few paces towards Mollie*) How long have you been married? Are you very much in love?

MOLLIE (*coldly*) We've been married just a year. (*Moving towards the stairs* L) Perhaps you'd like to go up and see your room?

CHRISTOPHER. Ticked off! (*He moves above the sofa table*) But I do so like knowing all about people. I mean, I think people are so madly interesting. Don't you?

MOLLIE. Well, I suppose some are and (*turning to Christopher*) some are not.

CHRISTOPHER. No, I don't agree. They're *all* interesting, because you never really know what anyone is like—or what they are really thinking. For instance, *you* don't know what *I'm* thinking about now, do you? (*He smiles as at some secret joke*)

MOLLIE. Not in the least. (*She moves down to the sofa table and takes a cigarette from the box*) Cigarette?

CHRISTOPHER. No, thank you. (*Moving to* R *of Mollie*) You see? The only people who really know what other people are like are artists—and they don't know why they know it! But if they're portrait painters (*he moves* C) it comes out—(*he sits on the right arm of the sofa*) on the canvas.

MOLLIE. Are you a painter? (*She lights her cigarette*)

CHRISTOPHER. No, I'm an architect. My parents, you know, baptized me Christopher, in the hope that I would be an architect. Christopher Wren! (*He laughs*) As good as halfway home. Actually, of course, everyone laughs about it and makes jokes about St Paul's. However—who knows?—I may yet have the last laugh.

(GILES *enters from the archway up* L *and crosses to the arch up* R)

Chris Wren's Prefab Nests may yet go down in history! (*To Giles*) I'm going to like it here. I find your wife *most* sympathetic.

GILES (*coldly*) Indeed.

CHRISTOPHER (*turning to look at Mollie*) And really very beautiful.

MOLLIE. Oh, don't be absurd.

(GILES *leans on the back of the large armchair*)

CHRISTOPHER. There, isn't that like an Englishwoman? Compliments always embarrass them. European women take compliments as a matter of course, but Englishwomen have all the feminine spirit crushed out of them by their husbands. (*He turns and looks at Giles*) There's something very boorish about English husbands.

MOLLIE (*hastily*) Come up and see your room. (*She crosses to the arch up* L)

CHRISTOPHER. Shall I?

MOLLIE (*to Giles*) Could you stoke up the hot water boiler?

(MOLLIE *and* CHRISTOPHER *exit up the stairs* L. GILES *scowls and crosses to* C. *The door bell peals. There is a pause then it peals several times impatiently.*

GILES *exits hurriedly up* R *to the front door. The sound of wind and snow is heard for a moment or two*)

MRS BOYLE (*off*) This *is* Monkswell Manor, I presume?

GILES (*off*) Yes . . .

(MRS BOYLE *enters through the archway up* R, *carrying a suitcase, some magazines and her gloves. She is a large, imposing woman in a very bad temper*)

MRS BOYLE. I am Mrs Boyle. (*She puts down the suitcase*)

GILES. I'm Giles Ralston. Come in to the fire, Mrs Boyle, and get warm.

(MRS BOYLE *moves down to the fire*)

Awful weather, isn't it? Is this your only luggage?

MRS BOYLE. A Major—Metcalf, is it?—is seeing to it.

GILES. I'll leave the door for him.

(GILES *goes out to the front door*)

MRS BOYLE. The taxi wouldn't risk coming up the drive.

(GILES *returns and comes down to* L *of Mrs Boyle*)

It stopped at the gate. We had to share a taxi from the station—

and there was great difficulty in getting *that*. (*Accusingly*) Nothing ordered to meet us, it seems.

GILES. I'm so sorry. We didn't know what train you would be coming by, you see, otherwise of course, we'd have seen that someone was—er—standing by.

MRS BOYLE. All trains should have been met.

GILES. Let me take your coat.

(MRS BOYLE *hands Giles her gloves and magazines. She stands by the fire warming her hands*)

My wife will be here in a moment. I'll just go along and give Metcalf a hand with the bags.

(GILES *exits up* R *to the front door*)

MRS BOYLE (*moving up to the arch as Giles goes*) The drive might at least have been cleared of snow. (*After his exit*) Most offhand and casual, I must say. (*She moves down to the fire and looks round her disapprovingly*)

(MOLLIE *hurries in from the stairs* L, *a little breathless*)

MOLLIE. I'm so sorry I . . .

MRS BOYLE. Mrs Ralston?

MOLLIE. Yes. I . . . (*She crosses to Mrs Boyle, half puts out her hand, then draws it back, uncertain of what guest house proprietors are supposed to do*)

(MRS BOYLE *surveys Mollie with displeasure*)

MRS BOYLE. You're very young.

MOLLIE. Young?

MRS BOYLE. To be running an establishment of this kind. You can't have had much experience.

MOLLIE (*backing away*) There has to be a beginning for everything, hasn't there?

MRS BOYLE. I see. Quite inexperienced. (*She looks round*) An old house. I hope you haven't got dry rot. (*She sniffs suspiciously*)

MOLLIE (*indignantly*) Certainly not!

MRS BOYLE. A lot of people don't know they have got dry rot until it's too late to do anything about it.

MOLLIE. The house is in perfect condition.

MRS BOYLE. H'm—it could do with a coat of paint. You know, you've got worm in this oak.

GILES (*off*) This way, Major.

(GILES *and* MAJOR METCALF *enter up* R. *Major Metcalf is a middle-aged, square-shouldered man, very military in manner and bearing.* GILES *moves up* C. MAJOR METCALF *puts down a suitcase he is carrying and moves above the armchair* C; MOLLIE *moves up to meet him*)

This is my wife.

Major Metcalf (*shaking hands with Mollie*) How d'you do? Absolute blizzard outside. Thought at one time we shouldn't make it. (*He sees Mrs Boyle*) Oh, I beg your pardon. (*He removes his hat*)

(Mrs Boyle *exits down* r)

If it goes on like this I should say you'll have five or six feet of snow by morning. (*He crosses to the fire*) Not seen anything like it since I was on leave in nineteen-forty.

Giles. I'll take these up. (*Picking up the cases. To Mollie*) Which rooms did you say? Blue Room and the Rose Room.

Mollie. No—I put Mr Wren in the Rose Room. He liked the fourposter so much. So it's Mrs Boyle in the Oak Room and Major Metcalf in the Blue Room.

Giles (*authoritatively*) Major! (*He moves* l *towards the stairs*)

Major Metcalf (*instinctively the soldier*) Sir!

(Major Metcalf *follows* Giles *and they exit up the stairs* l. Mrs Boyle *enters down* r *and moves up to the fireplace*)

Mrs Boyle. Do you have much servant difficulty here?

Mollie. We have quite a good local woman who comes in from the village.

Mrs Boyle. And what indoor staff?

Mollie. No indoor staff. Just us. (*She moves down to* l *of the armchair* c)

Mrs Boyle. In-deed. I understood this was a guest house in full running order.

Mollie. We're only just starting.

Mrs Boyle. I would have said that a proper staff of servants was essential before opening this kind of establishment. I consider your advertisement was most misleading. May I ask if I am the only guest—with Major Metcalf, that is?

Mollie. Oh no, there are several here.

Mrs Boyle. This weather, too. A blizzard (*she turns to the fire*) —no less—all very unfortunate.

Mollie. But we couldn't very well foresee the weather!

(Christopher Wren *enters quietly from the stairs* l *and comes up behind Mollie*)

Christopher (*singing*) "The North Wind doth blow
                    And it will bring snow
                    And what will the robin do then, poor
                        thing?"

I adore nursery rhymes, don't you? Always so tragic and *macabre*. That's why children like them.

Mollie. May I introduce. Mr Wren—Mrs Boyle.

(Christopher *bows*)

MRS BOYLE (*coldly*) How d'you do?

CHRISTOPHER. This is a *very* beautiful house. Don't you think so?

MRS BOYLE. I have come to the time of life when the amenities of an establishment are more important than its appearance.

(CHRISTOPHER *backs away up* R.
GILES *enters from the stairs* L *and stands below the arch*)

If I had not believed this was a running concern I should never have come here. I understand it was *fully* equipped with every home comfort.

GILES. There is no obligation for you to remain here if you are not satisfied, Mrs Boyle.

MRS BOYLE (*crossing to* R *of the sofa*) No, indeed, I should not think of doing so.

GILES. If there has been any misapprehension it would perhaps be better if you went elsewhere. I could ring up for the taxi to return. The roads are not yet blocked.

(CHRISTOPHER *moves down and sits in the armchair* C)

We have had so many applications for rooms that we shall be able to fill your place quite easily. In any case we are raising our terms next month.

MRS BOYLE. I am certainly not going to leave before I have tried what the place is like. You needn't think you can turn me out now.

(GILES *moves down* L)

Perhaps you will take me up to my bedroom, Mrs Ralston? (*She moves majestically towards the staircase* L)

MOLLIE. Certainly, Mrs Boyle. (*She follows Mrs Boyle. To Giles, softly, as she passes him*) Darling, you were wonderful . . .

(MRS BOYLE *and* MOLLIE *exit* L *up the stairs*)

CHRISTOPHER (*rising; childishly*) I think that's a perfectly horrible woman. I don't like her at all. I'd love to see you turn her out into the snow. Serve her right.

GILES. It's a pleasure I've got to forgo, I'm afraid.

(*The door bell peals*)

Lord, there's another of them.

(GILES *goes out to the front door*)

(*Off*) Come in—come in.

(CHRISTOPHER *moves to the sofa and sits.*
MISS CASEWELL *enters up* R. *She is a young woman of a manly type, and carries a case. She has a long dark coat, a light scarf and no hat.*
GILES *enters*)

MISS CASEWELL (*in a deep, manly voice*) Afraid my car's bogged about half a mile down the road—ran into a drift.

GILES. Let me take this. (*He takes her case and puts it R of the refectory table*) Any more stuff in the car?

MISS CASEWELL (*moving down to the fire*) No, I travel light.

(GILES *moves above the armchair* C)

Ha, glad to see you've got a good fire. (*She straddles in front of it in a manly fashion*)

GILES. Er—Mr Wren—Miss ——?

MISS CASEWELL. Casewell. (*She nods to Christopher*)

GILES. My wife will be down in a minute.

MISS CASEWELL. No hurry. (*She takes off her overcoat*) Got to get myself thawed out. Looks as though you're going to be snowed up here. (*Taking an evening paper from her overcoat pocket*) Weather forecast says heavy falls expected. Motorists warned, etcetera. Hope you've got plenty of provisions in.

GILES. Oh yes. My wife's an excellent manager. Anyway, we can always eat our hens.

MISS CASEWELL. Before we start eating each other, eh?

(*She laughs stridently and throws the overcoat at* GILES, *who catches it. She sits in the armchair* C)

CHRISTOPHER (*rising and crossing to the fire*) Any news in the paper—apart from the weather?

MISS CASEWELL. Usual political crisis. Oh yes, and a rather juicy murder!

CHRISTOPHER. A murder? (*Turning to Miss Casewell*) Oh, I *like* murder!

MISS CASEWELL (*handing him the paper*) They seem to think it was a homicidal maniac. Strangled a woman somewhere near Paddington. Sex maniac, I suppose. (*She looks at Giles*)

(GILES *crosses to* L *of the sofa table*)

CHRISTOPHER. Doesn't say much, does it? (*He sits in the small armchair* R *and reads*) "The police are anxious to interview a man seen in the vicinity of Culver Street at the time. Medium height, wearing darkish overcoat, lightish scarf and soft felt hat. Police messages to this effect have been broadcast throughout the day."

MISS CASEWELL. Useful description. Fit pretty well anyone, wouldn't it?

CHRISTOPHER. When it says that the police are anxious to interview someone, is that a polite way of hinting that he's the murderer?

MISS CASEWELL. Could be.

GILES. Who was the woman who was murdered?

CHRISTOPHER. Mrs Lyon. Mrs Maureen Lyon.

GILES. Young or old?

CHRISTOPHER. It doesn't say. It doesn't seem to have been robbery . . .

MISS CASEWELL (*to Giles*) I told you—sex maniac.

(MOLLIE *comes down the stairs and crosses to Miss Casewell*)

GILES. Here's Miss Casewell, Mollie. My wife.

MISS CASEWELL (*rising*) How d'you do? (*She shakes hands with Mollie vigorously*)

(GILES *picks up her case*)

MOLLIE. It's an awful night. Would you like to come up to your room? The water's hot if you'd like a bath.

MISS CASEWELL. You're right, I would.

(MOLLIE *and* MISS CASEWELL *exit to the stairs* L. GILES *follows them, carrying the case. Left alone,* CHRISTOPHER *rises and makes an exploration. He opens the door down* L, *peeps in and then exits. A moment or two later he reappears on the stairs* L. *He crosses to the arch up* R *and looks off. He sings "Little Jack Horner" and chuckles to himself, giving the impression of being slightly unhinged mentally. He moves behind the refectory table.*

GILES *and* MOLLIE *enter from the stairs* L, *talking.* CHRISTOPHER *hides behind the curtain.* MOLLIE *moves above the armchair* C *and* GILES *moves to the* R *end of the refectory table*)

MOLLIE. I must hurry out to the kitchen and get on with things. Major Metcalf is very nice. He won't be difficult. It's Mrs Boyle really frightens me. We *must* have a nice dinner. I was thinking of opening two tins of minced beef and cereal and a tin of peas, and mashing the potatoes. And there's stewed figs and custard. Do you think that will be all right?

GILES. Oh—I should think so. Not—not very original, perhaps.

CHRISTOPHER (*coming from behind the curtains and moving between Giles and Mollie*) Do let me help. I adore cooking. Why not an omelette? You've got eggs, haven't you?

MOLLIE. Oh yes, we've got plenty of eggs. We keep lots of fowls. They don't lay as well as they should but we've put down a lot of eggs.

(GILES *breaks away* L)

CHRISTOPHER. And if you've got a bottle of cheap, any type wine, you could add it to the—"minced beef and cereals", did you say? Give it a Continental flavour. Show me where the kitchen is and what you've got, and I daresay I shall have an inspiration.

MOLLIE. Come on.

(MOLLIE *and* CHRISTOPHER *exit through the archway* R *to the kitchen.* GILES *frowns, ejaculates something uncomplimentary to Chris-*

topher and crosses to the small armchair down R. *He picks up the newspaper and stands reading it with deep attention.*

He jumps as MOLLIE *returns to the room and speaks)*

Isn't he sweet? (*She moves above the sofa table*) He's put on an apron and he's getting all the things together. He says leave it all to him and don't come back for half an hour. If our guests want to do the cooking themselves, it will save a lot of trouble.

GILES. Why on earth did you give him the best room?

MOLLIE. I told you, he liked the fourposter.

GILES. He liked the pretty fourposter. Twerp!

MOLLIE. Giles!

GILES. I've got no use for that kind. (*Significantly*) *You* didn't handle his suitcase, I did.

MOLLIE. Had it got bricks in it? (*She crosses to the armchair* C *and sits*)

GILES. It was no weight at all. If you ask me there was *nothing* inside it. He's probably one of those young men who go about bilking hotel keepers.

MOLLIE. I don't believe it. I like him. (*She pauses*) I think Miss Casewell's rather peculiar, don't you?

GILES. Terrible female—if she *is* a female.

MOLLIE. It seems very hard that all our guests should be either unpleasant or odd. Anyway, I think Major Metcalf's all right, don't you?

GILES. Probably drinks!

MOLLIE. Oh, do you think so?

GILES. No, I don't. I was just feeling rather depressed. Well, at any rate we know the worst now. They've all arrived.

(*The door bell rings*)

MOLLIE. Who can that be?

GILES. Probably the Culver Street murderer.

MOLLIE (*rising*) Don't!

(GILES *exits up* R *to the front door.* MOLLIE *crosses to the fire*)

GILES (*off*) Oh.

(MR PARAVICINI *staggers in up* R, *carrying a small bag. He is foreign and dark and elderly with a rather flamboyant moustache. He is a slightly taller edition of Hercule Poirot, which may give a wrong impression to the audience. He wears a heavy fur-lined overcoat. He leans on the* L *side of the arch and puts down the bag.*

GILES *enters)*

PARAVICINI. A thousand pardons. I am—where am I?

GILES. This is Monkswell Manor Guest House.

PARAVICINI. But what stupendous good fortune! Madame! (*He moves down to Mollie, takes her hand and kisses it*)

(GILES *crosses above the armchair* C)

B

What an answer to prayer. A guest house—and a charming hostess. My Rolls Royce, alas, has run into a snowdrift. Blinding snow everywhere. I do not know where I am. Perhaps, I think to myself, I shall freeze to death. And then I take a little bag, I stagger through the snow, I see before me big iron gates. A habitation! I am saved. Twice I fall into the snow as I come up your drive, but at last I arrive and immediately—(*he looks round*) despair turns to joy. (*Changing his manner*) You can let me have a room—yes?

GILES. Oh yes . . .

MOLLIE. It's rather a small one, I'm afraid.

PARAVICINI. Naturally—naturally—you have other guests.

MOLLIE. We've only just opened this place as a guest house today, and so we're—we're rather new at it.

PARAVICINI (*leering at Mollie*) Charming—charming . . .

GILES. What about your luggage?

PARAVICINI. That is of no consequence. I have locked the car securely.

GILES. But wouldn't it be better to get it in?

PARAVICINI. No, no. (*He moves up to* R *of Giles*) I can assure you on such a night as this, there will be no thieves abroad. And for me, my wants are very simple. I have all I need—here—in this little bag. Yes, all that I need.

MOLLIE. You'd better get thoroughly warm.

(PARAVICINI *crosses to the fire*)

I'll see about your room. (*She moves to the armchair* C) I'm afraid it's rather a cold room because it faces north, but all the others are occupied.

PARAVICINI. You have several guests, then?

MOLLIE. There's Mrs Boyle and Major Metcalf and Miss Casewell and a young man called Christopher Wren—and now—you.

PARAVICINI. Yes—the unexpected guest. The guest that you did not invite. The guest who just arrived—from nowhere—out of the storm. It sounds quite dramatic, does it not? Who am I? You do not know. Where do I come from? You do not know. Me, I am the man of mystery. (*He laughs*)

(MOLLIE *laughs and looks at* GILES, *who grins feebly*. PARAVICINI *nods his head at Mollie in high good humour*)

But now, I tell you this. I complete the picture. From now on there will be no more arrivals. And no departures either. By tomorrow—perhaps even already—we are cut off from civilization. No butcher, no baker, no milkman, no postman, no daily papers—nobody and nothing but ourselves. That is admirable—admirable. It could not suit me better. My name, by the way, is Paravicini. (*He moves down to the small armchair* R)

Mollie. Oh yes. Ours is Ralston.

(Giles *moves to* l *of Mollie*)

Paravicini. Mr and Mrs Ralston? (*He nods his head as they agree. He looks round him and moves up to* r *of Mollie*) And this—is Monkswell Manor Guest House, you said? Good. Monkswell Manor Guest House. (*He laughs*) Perfect. (*He laughs*) Perfect. (*He laughs and crosses to the fireplace*)

Mollie *looks at* Giles *and they both look at Paravicini uneasily as*—

the Curtain *falls*

SCENE 2

Scene—*The same. The following afternoon.*

When the Curtain *rises it is not snowing, but snow can be seen banked high against the window.* Major Metcalf *is seated on the sofa reading a book, and* Mrs Boyle *is sitting in the large armchair* r *in front of the fire, writing on a pad on her knee.*

Mrs Boyle. I consider it *most* dishonest not to have told me they were only just starting this place.

Major Metcalf. Well, everything's got to have a beginning, you know. Excellent breakfast this morning. Good coffee. Scrambled eggs, home-made marmalade. And all nicely served, too. Little woman does it all herself.

Mrs Boyle. Amateurs—there should be a proper staff.

Major Metcalf. Excellent lunch, too.

Mrs Boyle. Cornbeef.

Major Metcalf. But very well disguised cornbeef. Red wine in it. Mrs Ralston promised to make a pie for us tonight.

Mrs Boyle (*rising and crossing to the radiator*) These radiators are not really hot. I shall speak about it.

Major Metcalf. Very comfortable beds, too. At least mine was. Hope yours was, too.

Mrs Boyle. It was quite adequate. (*She returns to the large armchair* r *and sits*) I don't quite see why the best bedroom should have been given to that *very* peculiar young man.

Major Metcalf. Got here ahead of us. First come, first served.

Mrs Boyle. From the advertisement I got *quite* a different impression of what this place would be like. A comfortable writing-room, and a much larger place altogether—with bridge and other amenities.

Major Metcalf. Regular old tabbies' delight.

MRS BOYLE. I beg your pardon.

MAJOR METCALF. Er—I mean, yes, I quite see what you mean.

(CHRISTOPHER *enters* L *from the stairs unnoticed*)

MRS BOYLE. No, indeed, *I* shan't stay here long.

CHRISTOPHER (*laughing*) No. No, I don't suppose you will.

(CHRISTOPHER *exits into the library up* L)

MRS POYLE. Really that is a very peculiar young man. Unbalanced mentally, I shouldn't wonder.

MAJOR METCALF. Think he's escaped from a lunatic asylum.

MRS BOYLE. I shouldn't be at all surprised.

(MOLLIE *enters through the archway up* R)

MOLLIE (*calling upstairs*) Giles?

GILES (*off*) Yes?

MOLLIE. Can you shovel the snow away again from the back door?

GILES (*off*) Coming.

(MOLLIE *disappears through the arch*)

MAJOR METCALF. I'll give you a hand, what? (*He rises and crosses up* R *to the arch*) Good exercise. Must have exercise.

(MAJOR METCALF *exits.*

GILES *enters from the stairs, crosses and exits up* R.

MOLLIE *returns, carrying a duster and a vacuum cleaner, crosses the Hall and runs upstairs.*

She collides with MISS CASEWELL *who is coming down the stairs*)

MOLLIE. Sorry!

MISS CASEWELL. That's all right.

(MOLLIE *exits.* MISS CASEWELL *comes slowly* C)

MRS BOYLE. Really! What an incredible young woman. Doesn't she know anything about housework? Carrying a carpet sweeper through the front hall. Aren't there any back stairs?

MISS CASEWELL (*taking a cigarette from a packet in her handbag*) Oh yes—nice back stairs. (*She crosses to the fire*) Very convenient if there was a fire. (*She lights the cigarette*)

MRS BOYLE. Then why not use them? Anyway, all the housework should have been done in the morning before lunch.

MISS CASEWELL. I gather our hostess had to cook the lunch.

MRS BOYLE. All very haphazard and amateurish. There should be a proper staff.

Miss Casewell. Not very easy to get nowadays, is it?

Mrs Boyle. No, indeed, the lower classes seem to have no idea of their responsibilities.

Miss Casewell. Poor old lower classes. Got the bit between their teeth, haven't they?

Mrs Boyle (*frostily*)　I gather you are a Socialist.

Miss Casewell. Oh, I wouldn't say that. I'm not a Red—just pale pink. (*She moves to the sofa and sits on the right arm*) But I don't take much interest in politics—I live abroad.

Mrs Boyle. I suppose conditions are much easier abroad.

Miss Casewell. I don't have to cook and clean—as I gather most people have to do in this country.

Mrs Boyle. This country has gone sadly downhill. Not what it used to be. I sold my house last year. Everything was too difficult.

Miss Casewell. Hotels and guest houses are easier.

Mrs Boyle. They certainly solve some of one's problems. Are you over in England for long?

Miss Casewell. Depends. I've got some business to see to. When it's done—I shall go back.

Mrs Boyle. To France?

Miss Casewell. No.

Mrs Boyle. Italy?

Miss Casewell. No. (*She grins*)

(Mrs Boyle *looks at her inquiringly but* Miss Casewell *does not respond.* Mrs Boyle *starts writing.* Miss Casewell *grins as she looks at her, crosses to the radio, turns it on, at first softly, then increases the volume*)

Mrs Boyle (*annoyed, as she is writing*)　Would you mind not having that on quite so loud! I always find the radio rather distracting when one is trying to write letters.

Miss Casewell. Do you?

Mrs Boyle. If you don't particularly want to listen just now . . .

Miss Casewell. It's my favourite music. There's a writing table in there. (*She nods towards the library door up* l)

Mrs Boyle. I know. But it's much warmer here.

Miss Casewell. Much warmer, I agree. (*She dances to the music*)

(Mrs Boyle, *after a moment's glare, rises and exits into the library up* l. Miss Casewell *grins, moves to the sofa table, and stubs out her cigarette. She moves up stage and picks up a magazine from the refectory table*)

Bloody old bitch. (*She moves to the large armchair and sits*)

(Christopher *enters from the library up* l *and moves down* l)

CHRISTOPHER. Oh!

MISS CASEWELL. Hullo.

CHRISTOPHER (*gesturing back to the library*) Wherever I go that woman seems to hunt me down—and then she glares at me—positively glares.

MISS CASEWELL (*indicating the radio*) Turn it down a bit.

(CHRISTOPHER *turns the radio down until it is playing quite softly*)

CHRISTOPHER. Is that all right?

MISS CASEWELL. Oh yes, it's served its purpose.

CHRISTOPHER. What purpose?

MISS CASEWELL. Tactics, boy.

(CHRISTOPHER *looks puzzled*. MISS CASEWELL *indicates the library*)

CHRISTOPHER. Oh, you mean *her*.

MISS CASEWELL. She'd pinched the best chair. I've got it now.

CHRISTOPHER. You drove her out. I'm glad. I'm very glad. I don't like her a bit. (*Crossing quickly to Miss Casewell*) Let's think of things we can do to annoy her, shall we? I wish she'd go away from here.

MISS CASEWELL. In this? Not a hope.

CHRISTOPHER. But when the snow melts.

MISS CASEWELL. Oh, when the snow melts lots of things may have happened.

CHRISTOPHER. Yes—yes—that's true. (*He goes to the window*) Snow's rather lovely, isn't it? So peaceful—and pure . . . It makes one forget things.

MISS CASEWELL. It doesn't make me forget.

CHRISTOPHER. How fierce you sound.

MISS CASEWELL. I was thinking.

CHRISTOPHER. What sort of thinking? (*He sits on the window seat*)

MISS CASEWELL. Ice on a bedroom jug, chilblains, raw and bleeding—one thin ragged blanket—a child shivering with cold and fear.

CHRISTOPHER. My dear, it sounds too, too grim—what is it? A novel?

MISS CASEWELL. You didn't know I was a writer, did you?

CHRISTOPHER. Are you? (*He rises and moves down to her*)

MISS CASEWELL. Sorry to disappoint you. Actually I'm not. (*She puts the magazine up in front of her face*)

(CHRISTOPHER *looks at her doubtfully, then crosses* L, *turns up the radio very loud and exits into the drawing-room. The telephone rings.*
      MOLLIE *runs down the stairs, duster in hand, and goes to the telephone*)

MOLLIE (*picking up the receiver*) Yes? (*She turns off the radio*) Yes—this is Monkswell Manor Guest House . . . What? . . . No, I'm afraid Mr Ralston can't come to the telephone just now. This is Mrs Ralston speaking. Who . . .? The Berkshire Police . . .?

(MISS CASEWELL *lowers her magazine*)

Oh yes, yes, Superintendent Hogben, I'm afraid that's impossible. He'd never get here. We're snowed up. Completely snowed up. The roads are impassable . . .

(MISS CASEWELL *rises and crosses to the arch up* L)

Nothing can get through . . . Yes . . . Very well . . . But what . . . Hullo—hullo . . . (*She replaces the receiver*)

(GILES *enters up* R *wearing an overcoat. He removes the overcoat and hangs it up in the hall*)

GILES. Mollie, do you know where there's another spade?

MOLLIE (*moving up* C) Giles, the police have just rung up.

MISS CASEWELL. Trouble with the police, eh? Serving liquor without a licence?

(MISS CASEWELL *exits* L *up the stairs*)

MOLLIE. They're sending out an inspector or a sergeant or something.

GILES (*moving to* R *of Mollie*) But he'll never get here.

MOLLIE. That's what I told them. But they seemed quite confident that he would.

GILES. Nonsense. Even a jeep couldn't get through today. Anyway, what's it all about?

MOLLIE. That's what I asked. But he wouldn't say. Just said I was to impress on my husband to listen very carefully to what Sergeant Trotter, I think it was, had to say, and to follow his instructions implicitly. Isn't it extraordinary?

GILES (*moving down to the fire*) What on earth do you think we've done?

MOLLIE (*moving to* L *of Giles*) Do you think it's those nylons from Gibraltar?

GILES. I did remember to get the wireless licence, didn't I?

MOLLIE. Yes, it's in the kitchen dresser.

GILES. I had rather a near shave with the car the other day but it was entirely the other fellow's fault.

MOLLIE. We must have done something . . .

GILES (*kneeling and putting a log on the fire*) Probably something to do with running this place. I expect we've ignored some tinpot regulation of some Ministry or other. You practically can't avoid it, nowadays. (*He rises and faces Mollie*)

MOLLIE. Oh dear, I wish we'd never started this place.

We're going to be snowed up for days, and everyone is cross, and we shall go through all our reserve of tins.

GILES. Cheer up, darling, (*he takes Mollie in his arms*) everything's going all right at the moment. I've filled up all the coalscuttles, and brought in the wood, and stoked the Aga and done the hens. I'll go and do the boiler next, and chop some kindling ... (*He breaks off*) You know, Mollie, (*he moves slowly up to* R *of the refectory table*) come to think of it, it must be something pretty serious to send a police sergeant trekking out in all this. It must be something really urgent ...

> (GILES *and* MOLLIE *look at each other uneasily.*
> MRS BOYLE *enters from the library up* L)

MRS BOYLE (*coming to* L *of the refectory table*) Ah, there you are, Mr Ralston. Do you know the central heating in the library is practically stone cold?

GILES. Sorry, Mrs Boyle, we're a bit short of coke and ...

MRS BOYLE. I am paying seven guineas a week here—seven guineas and I do not want to freeze.

GILES. I'll go and stoke it up.

> (GILES *exits by the archway up* R. MOLLIE *follows him to the arch*)

MRS BOYLE. Mrs Ralston, if you don't mind my saying so, that is a very extraordinary young man you have staying here. His manners—and his ties—and does he ever brush his hair?

MOLLIE. He's an extremely brilliant young architect.

MRS BOYLE. I beg your pardon?

MOLLIE. Christopher Wren is an architect ...

MRS BOYLE. My dear young woman, I have naturally heard of Sir Christopher Wren. (*She crosses to the fire*) Of course, he was an architect. He built St Paul's. You young people seem to think that no-one is educated but yourselves.

MOLLIE. I meant *this* Wren. His name is Christopher. His parents called him that because they hoped he'd be an architect. (*She crosses to the sofa table and takes a cigarette from the box*) And he is—or nearly one—so it turned out all right.

MRS BOYLE. Humph. Sounds a fishy story to me. (*She sits in the large armchair*) I should make some inquiries about him if I were you. What do you know of him?

MOLLIE. Just as much as I know about you, Mrs Boyle— which is that you are both paying us seven guineas a week. (*She lights her cigarette*) That is really all I need to know, isn't it? And all that concerns me. It doesn't matter to me whether I like my guests, or whether (*meaningly*) I don't.

MRS BOYLE. You are young and inexperienced and should welcome advice from someone more knowledgeable than yourself. And what about this foreigner?

MOLLIE. What about him?

MRS BOYLE. You weren't expecting him, were you?

MOLLIE. To turn away a *bona fide* traveller is against the law, Mrs Boyle. *You* should know that.

MRS BOYLE. Why do you say that?

MOLLIE (*moving down* C) Weren't you a magistrate, sitting on the bench, Mrs Boyle?

MRS BOYLE. All I say is that this Paravicini, or whatever he calls himself, seems to me . . .

(PARAVICINI *enters softly from the stairs* L)

PARAVICINI. Beware, dear lady. You talk of the devil and here he is. Ha, ha.

(MRS BOYLE *jumps*)

MRS BOYLE. I didn't hear you come in.

(MOLLIE *moves behind the sofa table*)

PARAVICINI. I came in on tiptoe—like this. (*He demonstrates, moving down* C) Nobody ever hears me if I do not want them to. I find that very amusing.

MRS BOYLE. Indeed?

PARAVICINI (*sitting in the armchair* C) Now there was a young lady . . .

MRS BOYLE (*rising*) Well, I must get on with my letters. I'll see if it's a little warmer in the drawing-room.

(MRS BOYLE *exits to the drawing-room down* L. MOLLIE *follows her to the door*)

PARAVICINI. My charming hostess looks upset. What is it, dear lady? (*He leers at her*)

MOLLIE. Everything's rather difficult this morning. Because of the snow.

PARAVICINI. Yes. Snow makes things difficult, does it not? (*He rises*) Or else it makes them easy. (*He moves up to the refectory table and sits*) Yes—very easy.

MOLLIE. I don't know what you mean.

PARAVICINI. No, there is quite a lot you do not know. I think, for one thing, that you do not know very much about running a guest house.

MOLLIE (*moving to* L *of the sofa table and stubbing out her cigarette*) I daresay we don't. But we mean to make a go of it.

PARAVICINI. Bravo—bravo! (*He claps his hands and rises*)

MOLLIE. I'm not such a very bad cook . . .

PARAVICINI (*leering*) You are without doubt an enchanting cook. (*He moves behind the sofa table and takes Mollie's hand*)

(MOLLIE *draws it away and moves below the sofa down* C)

May I give you a little word of warning, Mrs Ralston? (*Moving below the sofa*) You and your husband must not be too trusting, you know. Have you references with these guests of yours?

MOLLIE. Is that usual? (*She turns to Paravicini*) I always thought people just—just *came?*

PARAVICINI. It is advisable to know a little about the people who sleep under your roof. Take, for example, myself. I turn up saying that my car is overturned in a snowdrift. What do you know of me? Nothing at all! I may be a thief, a robber, (*he moves slowly towards Mollie*) a fugitive from justice—a madman—even —a murderer.

MOLLIE (*backing away*) Oh!

PARAVICINI. You see! And perhaps you know just as little of your other guests.

MOLLIE. Well, as far as Mrs Boyle goes . . .

(MRS BOYLE *enters from the drawing-room.* MOLLIE *moves up* C *to the refectory table*)

MRS BOYLE. The drawing-room is far too cold to sit in. I shall write my letters in here. (*She crosses to the large armchair*)

PARAVICINI. Allow me to poke the fire for you. (*He moves* R *and does so*)

(MAJOR METCALF *enters up* R *through the archway*)

MAJOR METCALF (*to Mollie; with old-fashioned modesty*) Mrs Ralston, is your husband about? I'm afraid the pipes of the—er —the downstairs cloakroom are frozen.

MOLLIE. Oh dear. What an awful day. First the police and then the pipes. (*She moves to the arch up* R)

(PARAVICINI *drops the poker with a clatter.* MAJOR METCALF *stands as though paralysed*)

MRS BOYLE (*startled*) Police?

MAJOR METCALF (*loudly, as if incredulous*) Police, did you say? (*He moves to the* L *end of the refectory table*)

MOLLIE. They rang up. Just now. To say they're sending a sergeant out here. (*She looks at the snow*) But I don't think he'll ever get here.

(GILES *enters from the archway up* R *with a basket of logs*)

GILES. The ruddy coke's more than half stones. And the price . . . Hullo, is anything the matter?

MAJOR METCALF. I hear the police are on their way here. Why?

GILES. Oh, that's all right. No-one can get through in this. Why, the drifts must be five feet deep. The roads are all banked up. Nobody will get here today. (*He takes the logs to the fireplace*) Excuse me, Mr Paravicini. May I put these down.

(PARAVICINI *moves down stage of the fireplace.*
   There are three sharp taps on the window as SERGEANT TROTTER *presses his face to the pane and peers in.* MOLLIE *gives a cry and points.* GILES *crosses and throws open the window.* SERGEANT TROTTER *is on skis and is a cheerful, commonplace young man with a slight cockney accent*)

TROTTER. Are you Mr Ralston?
GILES. Yes.
TROTTER. Thank you, sir. Detective Sergeant Trotter. Berkshire Police. Can I get these skis off and stow them somewhere?
GILES (*pointing* R) Go round that way to the front door. I'll meet you.
TROTTER. Thank you, sir.

(GILES *leaves the window open and exits to the front door up* R)

MRS BOYLE. I suppose that's what we pay our police force for, nowadays, to go round enjoying themselves at winter sports.

(MOLLIE *crosses below the refectory table to the window*)

PARAVICINI (*moving up to* C *of the refectory table; in a fierce whisper to Mollie*) Why did you send for the police, Mrs Ralston?
MOLLIE. But I didn't. (*She shuts the window*)

(CHRISTOPHER *enters from the drawing-room* L *and comes to* L O, *the sofa.* PARAVICINI *moves to the* R *end of the refectory table*)

CHRISTOPHER. Who's that man? Where did he come from? He passed the drawing-room window on skis. All over snow and looking terribly hearty.
MRS BOYLE. You may believe it or not, but that man is a policeman. A policeman—ski-ing!

(GILES *and* TROTTER *enter from the front door.* TROTTER *has removed his skis and is carrying them*)

GILES (*moving* R *of the arch up* R) Er—this is Detective Sergeant Trotter.
TROTTER (*moving to* L *of the large armchair*) Good afternoon.
MRS BOYLE. You can't be a sergeant. You're too young.
TROTTER. I'm not quite as young as I look, madam.
CHRISTOPHER. But terribly hearty.
GILES. We'll stow your skis away under the stairs.

(GILES *and* TROTTER *exit through the archway up* R)

MAJOR METCALF. Excuse me, Mrs Ralston, but may I use your telephone?
MOLLIE. Of course, Major Metcalf.

(MAJOR METCALF *goes to the telephone and dials*)

CHRISTOPHER (*sitting at the* R *end of the sofa*) He's very attractive, don't you think so? I always think that policemen are very attractive.

Mrs Boyle. No brains. You can see that at a glance.

Major Metcalf (*into the telephone*) Hullo! Hullo! . . . (*To Mollie*) Mrs Ralston, this telephone is dead—quite dead.

Mollie. It was all right about half an hour ago.

Major Metcalf. The line's gone with the weight of the snow, I suppose.

Christopher (*laughing hysterically*) So we're quite cut off now. Quite cut off. That's funny, isn't it?

Major Metcalf (*moving to L of the sofa*) I don't see anything to laugh at.

Mrs Boyle. No, indeed.

Christopher. Ah, it's a private joke of my own. Hist, the sleuth is returning.

(Trotter *enters from the archway up* R, *followed by* Giles. Trotter *moves down* C *while* Giles *crosses to* L *of the sofa table*)

Trotter (*taking out his notebook*) Now we can get to business, Mr Ralston. Mrs Ralston?

(Mollie *moves down* C)

Giles. Do you want to see us alone? If so, we can go into the library. (*He points towards the library door up* L)

Trotter (*turning his back to the audience*) It's not necessary, sir. It'll save time if everybody's present. If I might sit at this table? (*He moves up to the* R *end of the refectory table*)

Paravicini. I beg your pardon. (*He moves behind the table to the* L *end*)

Trotter. Thank you. (*He settles himself in a judicial manner* C *behind the refectory table*)

Mollie. Oh, do hurry up and tell us. (*She moves up to the* R *end of the refectory table*) What have we done?

Trotter (*surprised*) Done? Oh, it's nothing of *that* kind, Mrs Ralston. It's something quite different. It's more a matter of police protection, if you understand me.

Mollie. Police protection?

Trotter. It relates to the death of Mrs Lyon—Mrs Maureen Lyon of twenty-four Culver Street, London, West two, who was murdered yesterday, the fifteenth instant. You may have heard or read about the case?

Mollie. Yes. I heard it on the wireless. The woman who was strangled?

Trotter. That's right, madam. (*To Giles*) The first thing I want to know is if you were acquainted with this Mrs Lyon.

Giles. Never heard of her.

(Mollie *shakes her head*)

Trotter. You mayn't have known of her under the name of Lyon. Lyon wasn't her real name. She had a police record and her fingerprints were on file so we were able to identify her without difficulty. Her real name was Maureen Stanning. Her husband was a farmer, John Stanning, who resided at Longridge Farm not very far from here.

Giles. Longridge Farm! Wasn't that where those children . . .?

Trotter. Yes, the Longridge Farm case.

(Miss Casewell *enters from the stairs* L)

Miss Casewell. Three children . . . (*She crosses to the armchair down* R *and sits*)

(*Everyone watches her*)

Trotter. That's right, miss. The Corrigans. Two boys and a girl. Brought before the court as in need of care and protection. A home was found for them with Mr and Mrs Stanning at Longridge Farm. One of the children subsequently died as the result of criminal neglect and persistent ill-treatment. Case made a bit of a sensation at the time.

Mollie (*very much shaken*) It was horrible.

Trotter. The Stannings were sentenced to terms of imprisonment. Stanning died in prison. Mrs Stanning served her sentence and was duly released. Yesterday, as I say, she was found strangled at twenty-four Culver Street.

Mollie. Who did it?

Trotter. I'm coming to that, madam. A notebook was picked up near the scene of the crime. In that notebook was written two addresses. One was twenty-four Culver Street. The other (*he pauses*) was Monkswell Manor.

Giles. What?

Trotter. Yes, sir.

(*During the next speech* Paravicini *moves slowly* L *to the stairs and leans on the upstage side of the arch*)

That's why Superintendent Hogben, on receiving this information from Scotland Yard, thought it imperative for me to come out here and find out if you knew of any connexion between this house, or anyone in this house, and the Longridge Farm case.

Giles (*moving to the* L *end of the refectory table*) There's nothing—absolutely nothing. It must be a coincidence.

Trotter. Superintendent Hogben doesn't think it is a coincidence, sir.

(Major Metcalf *turns and looks at Trotter. During the next speeches he takes out his pipe and fills it*)

He'd have come himself if it had been in any way possible. Under the weather conditions, and as I can ski, he sent me with instructions to get full particulars of everyone in the house, to report back to him by phone, and to take what measures I thought fit to ensure the safety of the household.

GILES. Safety? What danger does he think we're in? Good Lord, he's not suggesting that somebody is going to be killed here.

TROTTER. I don't want to frighten any of the ladies—but frankly, yes, that is the idea.

GILES. But—why?

TROTTER. That's what I'm here to find out.

GILES. But the whole thing's crazy!

TROTTER. Yes, sir. It's because it's crazy that it's dangerous.

MRS BOYLE. Nonsense!

MISS CASEWELL. I must say it seems a bit far-fetched.

CHRISTOPHER. I think it's wonderful. (*He turns and looks at Major Metcalf*)

(MAJOR METCALF *lights his pipe*)

MOLLIE. Is there something that you haven't told us, Sergeant?

TROTTER. Yes, Mrs Ralston. Below the two addresses was written "Three Blind Mice". And on the dead woman's body was a paper with "This is the First" written on it, and below the words, a drawing of three little mice and a bar of music. The music was the tune of the nursery rhyme *Three Blind Mice*. You know how it goes. (*He sings*) "Three Blind Mice . . ."

MOLLIE (*singing*)   "Three Blind Mice,
                  See how they run,
                  They all ran after the farmer's wife . . ."

Oh, it's horrible.

GILES. There were three children and one died?

TROTTER. Yes, the youngest, a boy of eleven.

GILES. What happened to the other two?

TROTTER. The girl was adopted by someone. We haven't been able to trace her present whereabouts. The elder boy would now be about twenty-two. Deserted from the Army and has not been heard of since. According to the Army psychologist, was definitely schizophrenic. (*Explaining*) A bit queer in the head, that's to say.

MOLLIE. They think that it was he who killed Mrs Lyon— Mrs Stanning? (*She moves down to the armchair* c)

TROTTER. Yes.

MOLLIE. And that he's a homicidal maniac (*she sits*) and that he will turn up here and try to kill someone—but why?

TROTTER. That's what I've got to find out from you. As the Superintendent sees it, there must be some connexion. (*To Giles*) Now you state, sir, that you yourself have never had any connexion with the Longridge Farm case?

GILES. No.

Trotter. And the same goes for you, madam?

Mollie (*not at ease*) I—no—I mean—no connexion.

Trotter. What about servants?

(Mrs Boyle *registers disapproval*)

Mollie. We haven't got any servants. (*She rises and moves up* R *to the arch*) That reminds me. Would you mind, Sergeant Trotter, if I went to the kitchen? I'll be there if you want me.

Trotter. That's quite all right, Mrs Ralston.

(Mollie *exits by the archway up* R. Giles *crosses up* R *to the arch, but he is stopped as* Trotter *speaks*)

Now can I have all your names, please?

Mrs Boyle. This is quite ridiculous. We are merely staying in a kind of hotel. We only arrived yesterday. We've nothing to do with this place.

Trotter. You'd planned to come here in advance, though. You'd booked your rooms here ahead.

Mrs Boyle. Well, yes. All except Mr ——? (*She looks at Paravicini*)

Paravicini. Paravicini. (*He moves to the* L *end of the refectory table*) My car overturned in a snowdrift.

Trotter. I see. What I'm getting at is that anyone who's been following you around might know very well that you were coming here. Now, there's just one thing I want to know and I want to know it quick. Which one of you is it that has some connexion with that business at Longridge Farm?

(*There is a dead silence*)

You're not being very sensible, you know. One of you is in danger —deadly danger. I've got to know which one that is.

(*There is another silence*)

All right, I'll ask you one by one. (*To Paravicini*) You, first, since you seem to have arrived here more or less by accident, Mr Pari——?

Paravicini. Para— Paravicini. But, my dear Inspector, I know nothing, but nothing of what you have been talking about. I am a stranger in this country. I know nothing of these local affairs of bygone years.

Trotter (*rising and moving down to* L *of Mrs Boyle*) Mrs—— ?

Mrs Boyle. Boyle. I don't see—really I consider it an impertinence . . . Why on earth should *I* have anything to do with such—this distressing business?

(Major Metcalf *looks sharply at her*)

Trotter (*looking at Miss Casewell*) Miss——?

MISS CASEWELL (*slowly*)   Casewell. Leslie Casewell. I never heard of Longridge Farm, and I know nothing about it.

TROTTER (*moving to* R *of the sofa; to Major Metcalf*)   You, sir?

MAJOR METCALF. Metcalf—Major. Read about the case in the papers at the time. I was stationed at Edinburgh then. No personal knowledge.

TROTTER (*to Christopher*)   And you?

CHRISTOPHER. Christopher Wren. I was a mere child at the time. I don't remember even hearing about it.

TROTTER (*moving behind the sofa table*)   And that's all you have to say—any of you?

(*There is a silence*)

(*Moving* C)   Well, if one of you gets murdered, you'll have yourself to blame. Now then, Mr Ralston, can I have a look round the house?

(TROTTER *exits up* R *with* GILES. PARAVICINI *sits at the window seat*)

CHRISTOPHER (*rising*)   My dears, how melodramatic. He's very attractive, isn't he? (*He moves up to the refectory table*) I do admire the police. So stern and hardboiled. Quite a thrill, this whole business. *Three Blind Mice.* How does the tune go? (*He whistles or hums it*)

MRS BOYLE. Really, Mr Wren!

CHRISTOPHER. Don't you like it? (*He moves to* L *of Mrs Boyle*) But it's a signature tune—the signature of the murderer. Just fancy what a kick he must be getting out of it.

MRS BOYLE. Melodramatic rubbish. I don't believe a word of it.

CHRISTOPHER (*stalking behind her*)   But just wait, Mrs Boyle. Till I creep up behind you, and you feel my hands on your throat.

MRS BOYLE. Stop . . . (*She rises*)

MAJOR METCALF. That'll do, Christopher. It's a poor joke, anyway. In fact, it's not a joke at all.

CHRISTOPHER. Oh, but it *is*! (*He moves above the armchair* C) That's just what it is. A madman's joke. That's just what makes it so deliciously *macabre*. (*He moves up* R *to the archway, looks round and giggles*) If you could just see your faces!

(CHRISTOPHER *exits through the archway*)

MRS BOYLE (*moving up* R *to the arch*)   A singularly ill-mannered and neurotic young man.

(MOLLIE *enters from the dining-room down* R *and stands by the door*)

MOLLIE. Where's Giles?

Miss Casewell. Taking our policeman on a conducted tour of the house.

Mrs Boyle (*moving down to the large armchair*) Your friend, the architect, has been behaving in a most abnormal manner.

Major Metcalf. Young fellows seem nervy nowadays. Daresay he'll grow out of it.

Mrs Boyle (*sitting*) Nerves? I've no patience with people who say they have nerves. *I* haven't any nerves.

(Miss Casewell *rises and crosses to the stairs* L)

Major Metcalf. No? Perhaps that's just as well for you, Mrs Boyle.

Mrs Boyle. What do you mean?

Major Metcalf (*moving to* L *of the armchair* C) I think you were actually one of the magistrates on the Bench at the time. In fact, you were responsible for sending those three children to Longridge Farm.

Mrs Boyle. Really, Major Metcalf. I can hardly be held responsible. We had reports from welfare workers. The farm people seemed very nice and were most anxious to have the children. It seemed most satisfactory. Eggs and fresh milk and a healthy out-of-doors life.

Major Metcalf. Kicks, blows, starvation, and a thoroughly vicious couple.

Mrs Boyle. But how was I to know? They were very civilly spoken.

Mollie. Yes, I was right. (*She moves up* C *and stares at Mrs Boyle*) It *was* you . . .

(Major Metcalf *looks sharply at Mollie*)

Mrs Boyle. One tries to do a public duty and all one gets is abuse.

(Paravicini *laughs heartily*)

Paravicini. You must forgive me, but indeed I find all this most amusing. I enjoy myself greatly..

(*Still laughing,* Paravicini *exits down* L *to the drawing-room.* Mollie *moves to* R *of the sofa*)

Mrs Boyle. I never did like that man!

Miss Casewell (*moving to* L *of the sofa table*) Where did he come from last night? (*She takes a cigarette from the box*)

Mollie. I don't know.

Miss Casewell. Looks a bit of a spiv to me. Makes his face up, too. Rouge and powder. Disgusting. He must be quite old, too. (*She lights the cigarette*)

Mollie. And yet he skips about as though he were quite young.

C

MAJOR METCALF. You'll be wanting more wood. I'll get it.

(MAJOR METCALF *exits up* R)

MOLLIE. It's almost dark and yet it's only four in the afternoon. I'll turn the lights on. (*She moves down* R *and switches on the wall brackets over the fireplace*) That's better.

(*There is a pause.* MRS BOYLE *glances uncomfortably first at* MOLLIE *and then at* MISS CASEWELL, *who are both watching her*)

MRS BOYLE (*assembling her writing things*) Now where did I leave my pen? (*She rises and crosses* L)

(MRS BOYLE *exits up* L *to the library. There is the sound of a piano being played from the drawing-room—the tune of "Three Blind Mice" picked out with one finger*)

MOLLIE (*moving up to the window to close the curtains*) What a horrid little tune that is.

MISS CASEWELL. Don't you like it? Reminds you of your childhood perhaps—an unhappy childhood?

MOLLIE. I was very happy as a child. (*She moves round to* C *of the refectory table*)

MISS CASEWELL. You were lucky.

MOLLIE. Weren't you happy?

MISS CASEWELL (*crossing to the fire*) No.

MOLLIE. I'm sorry.

MISS CASEWELL. But all that's a long time ago. One gets over things.

MOLLIE. I suppose so.

MISS CASEWELL. Or doesn't one? Damned hard to say.

MOLLIE. They say that what happened when you're a child matters more than anything else.

MISS CASEWELL. They say—they say. Who says?

MOLLIE. Psychologists.

MISS CASEWELL. All humbug. Just a damned lot of nonsense. I've no use for psychologists and psychiatrists.

MOLLIE (*moving down below the sofa*) I've never really had much to do with them.

MISS CASEWELL. A good thing for you you haven't. It's all a lot of hooey—the whole thing. Life's what you make of it. Go straight ahead—don't look back.

MOLLIE. One can't always help looking back.

MISS CASEWELL. Nonsense. It's a question of will power.

MOLLIE. Perhaps.

MISS CASEWELL (*forcefully*) I *know*. (*She moves down* C)

MOLLIE. I expect you're right . . . (*She sighs*) But sometimes things happen—to make you remember . . .

MISS CASEWELL. Don't give in. Turn your back on them.

MOLLIE. Is that really the right way? I wonder. Perhaps that's all wrong. Perhaps one ought really to—face them.

MISS CASEWELL. Depends what you're talking about.

MOLLIE (*with a slight laugh*) Sometimes, I hardly know what I am talking about. (*She sits on the sofa*)

MISS CASEWELL (*moving to Mollie*) Nothing from the past is going to affect me—except in the way I want it to.

(GILES *and* TROTTER *enter from the stairs* L)

TROTTER. Well, everything's all right upstairs. (*He looks at the open dining-room door, crosses and exits into the dining-room. He reappears in the archway up* R)

(MISS CASEWELL *exits into the dining-room, leaving the door open.* MOLLIE *rises and begins to tidy up, rearranging the cushions, then moves up to the curtains.* GILES *moves up to* L *of Mollie.* TROTTER *crosses down* L)

(*Opening the door down* L) What's in here, drawing-room?

(*The sound of the piano is heard much louder while the door is open.* TROTTER *exits into the drawing-room and shuts the door. Presently he reappears at the door up* L)

MRS BOYLE (*off*) Would you mind shutting that door. This place is full of draughts.

TROTTER. Sorry, madam, but I've got to get the lay of the land.

(TROTTER *closes the door and exits up the stairs.* MOLLIE *moves above the armchair* C)

GILES (*coming down to* L *of Mollie*) Mollie, what's all this . . .?

(TROTTER *reappears down the stairs*)

TROTTER. Well, that completes the tour. Nothing suspicious. I think I'll make my report now to Superintendent Hogben. (*He goes to the telephone*)

MOLLIE (*moving to* L *of the refectory table*) But you can't telephone. The line's dead . . .

TROTTER (*swinging round sharply*) What? (*He picks up the receiver*) Since when?

MOLLIE. Major Metcalf tried it just after you arrived.

TROTTER. But it was all right earlier. Superintendent Hogben got through all right.

MOLLIE. Oh yes. I suppose, since then, the lines are down with the snow.

TROTTER. I wonder. It may have been *cut*. (*He puts the receiver down and turns to them*)

GILES. Cut? But who could cut it?

TROTTER. Mr Ralston . . . Just how much do you know about these people who are staying in your guest house?

GILES. I—we—we don't really know anything about them.

TROTTER. Ah. (*He moves above the sofa table*)

GILES (*moving to* R *of Trotter*) Mrs Boyle wrote from a Bournemouth hotel, Major Metcalf from an address in—where was it?

MOLLIE. Leamington. (*She moves to* L *of Trotter*)

GILES. Wren wrote from Hampstead and the Casewell woman from a private hotel in Kensington. Paravicini, as we've told you, turned up out of the blue last night. Still, I suppose they've all got ration books—that sort of thing.

TROTTER. I shall go into all that, of course. But there's not much reliance to be placed on that sort of evidence.

MOLLIE. But even if this—this maniac is trying to get here and kill us all—or one of us, we're quite safe now. Because of the snow. No-one can get here till it melts.

TROTTER. Unless he's here already.

GILES. Here already?

TROTTER. Why not, Mr Ralston? All these people arrived here yesterday evening. Some hours after the murder of Mrs Stanning. Plenty of time to get here.

GILES. But except for Mr Paravicini, they'd all booked beforehand.

TROTTER. Well, why not? These crimes were planned.

GILES. Crimes? There's only been one crime. In Culver Street. Why are you sure there will be another here?

TROTTER. That it will happen here, no—I hope to prevent that. That it will be attempted, yes.

GILES (*crossing to the fire*) I can't believe it. It's so fantastic.

TROTTER. It isn't fantastic. It's just facts.

MOLLIE. You've got a description of what this—man looked like in London?

TROTTER. Medium height, indeterminate build, darkish overcoat, soft felt hat, face hidden by a muffler. Spoke in a whisper. (*He crosses to* L *of the armchair* C. *He pauses*) There are three darkish overcoats hanging up in the hall now. One of them is yours, Mr Ralston . . . There are three lightish felt hats . . .

(GILES *starts to move towards the arch up* R *but he stops when Mollie speaks*)

MOLLIE. I still can't believe it.

TROTTER. You see? It's this telephone wire that worries me. If it's been cut . . . (*He crosses to the phone, bends down and studies the wire*)

MOLLIE. I must go and get on with the vegetables.

(MOLLIE *exits through the archway up* R. GILES *picks up Mollie's glove from the armchair* C *and holds it absently, smoothing it out. He extracts a London bus ticket from the glove—stares at it—then after Mollie—then back to the ticket*)

TROTTER. Is there an extension?

(GILES *frowns at the bus ticket, and does not answer*)

GILES. I beg your pardon. Did you say something?

TROTTER. Yes, Mr Ralston, I said "Is there an extension?" (*He crosses to* C)

GILES. Yes, up in our bedroom.

TROTTER. Go and try it up there for me, will you?

(GILES *exits to the stairs, carrying the glove and bus ticket and looking dazed.* TROTTER *continues to trace the wire to the window. He pulls back the curtain and opens the window, trying to follow the wire. He crosses to the arch up* R, *goes out and returns with a torch. He moves to the window, jumps out and bends down, looking, then disappears out of sight. It is practically dark.*

MRS BOYLE *enters from the library up* L, *shivers and notices the open window*)

MRS BOYLE (*moving to the window*) Who's left this window open? (*She shuts the window and closes the curtain, then moves to the fire and puts another log on it. She crosses to the radio and turns it on. She moves up to the refectory table, picks up a magazine and looks at it*)

(*There is a music programme on the radio.* MRS BOYLE *frowns, moves to the radio and tunes in to a different programme*)

VOICE ON THE RADIO. . . . to understand what I may term as the mechanics of fear, you have to study the precise effect produced on the human mind. Imagine, for instance, that you are alone in a room. It is late in the afternoon. A door opens softly behind you . . .

(*The door down* R *opens. The tune of "Three Blind Mice" is heard whistled.* MRS BOYLE *turns with a start*)

MRS BOYLE (*with relief*) Oh, it's *you*. I can't find any programme worth listening to. (*She moves to the radio and tunes in to the music programme*)

(*A hand shows through the open doorway and clicks the light switch. The lights suddenly go out*)

Here—what are you doing? Why did you turn out the light?

(*The radio is at full volume, and through it are heard gurgles and a scuffle.* MRS BOYLE's *body falls.*

MOLLIE *enters by the archway up* R *and stands perplexed*)

MOLLIE. Why is it all dark? What a noise!

She switches on the lights at the switch up R *and crosses to the radio to turn it down. Then she sees Mrs Boyle lying strangled in front of the sofa and screams as—*

the CURTAIN *quickly falls*

ACT II

SCENE—*The same. Ten minutes later.*

When the CURTAIN *rises, Mrs Boyle's body has been removed and every-one is assembled in the room.* TROTTER *is in charge and is sitting on the upstage side of the refectory table.* MOLLIE *is standing at the* R *end of the refectory table. The others are all sitting;* MAJOR METCALF *in the large armchair* R, CHRISTOPHER *in the desk chair,* GILES *on the stairs* L, MISS CASEWELL *at the* R *end of the sofa, and* PARAVICINI *at the* L *end.*

TROTTER. Now, Mrs Ralston, try and think—*think* . . .

MOLLIE (*at breaking point*) I can't think. My head's numbed.

TROTTER. Mrs Boyle had only just been killed when you got to her. You came from the kitchen. Are you sure you didn't see or hear anybody as you came along the hallway?

MOLLIE. No—no, I don't think so. Just the radio blaring out in here. I couldn't think who'd turned it on so loud. I wouldn't hear anything else with that, would I?

TROTTER. That was clearly the murderer's idea—or (*meaningly*) murderess.

MOLLIE. How could I hear anything else?

TROTTER. You might have done. If the murderer had left the Hall that way (*he points* L) he might have heard you coming from the kitchen. He might have slipped up the back stairs—or into the dining-room . . .

MOLLIE. I think—I'm not sure—I heard a door creak—and shut—just as I came out of the kitchen.

TROTTER. Which door?

MOLLIE. I don't know.

TROTTER. Think, Mrs Ralston—try and *think*. Upstairs? Downstairs? Close at hand? Right? Left?

MOLLIE (*tearful*) I don't know, I tell you. I'm not even sure I heard anything. (*She moves down to the armchair* C *and sits*)

GILES (*rising and moving to* L *of the refectory table; angrily*) Can't you stop bullying her? Can't you see she's all in?

TROTTER (*sharply*) We're investigating a murder, Mr Ralston. Up to now, nobody has taken this thing seriously. Mrs Boyle didn't. She held out on me with information. You all held out on me. Well, Mrs Boyle is dead. Unless we get to the bottom of this —and quickly, mind—there may be another death.

GILES. Another? Nonsense. Why?

TROTTER (*gravely*) Because there were *three* little blind mice.

GILES. A death for each of them? But there would have to be

34

some connexion—I mean another connexion—with the Long-ridge Farm business.

TROTTER. Yes, there would have to be that.

GILES. But why another death *here*?

TROTTER. Because there were only two addresses in the note-book we found. Now, at twenty-four Culver Street there was only one possible victim. She's dead. But here at Monkswell Manor there is a wider field. (*He looks round the circle meaningly*)

MISS CASEWELL. Nonsense. Surely it would be a most unlikely coincidence that there should be *two* people brought here by chance, both of them with a share in the Longridge Farm case?

TROTTER. Given certain circumstances, it wouldn't be so much of a coincidence. Think it out, Miss Casewell. (*He rises*) Now I want to get down quite clearly where everyone was when Mrs Boyle was killed. I've already got Mrs Ralston's statement. You were in the kitchen preparing vegetables. You came out of the kitchen, along the passage, through the swing door into the hall and in here. (*He points to the archway* R) The radio was blaring, but the light was switched off, and the hall was dark. You switched the light on, saw Mrs Boyle, and screamed.

MOLLIE. Yes. I screamed and screamed. And at last—people came.

TROTTER (*moving down to* L *of Mollie*) Yes. As you say, people came—a lot of people from different directions—all arriving more or less at once. (*He pauses, moves down* C *and turns his back to the audience*) Now then, when I got out of that window (*he points*) to trace the telephone wire, *you*, Mr Ralston, went upstairs to the room you and Mrs Ralston occupy, to try the extension telephone. (*Moving up* C) Where were you when Mrs Ralston screamed?

GILES. I was still up in the bedroom. The extension telephone was dead, too. I looked out of the window to see if I could see any sign of the wires being cut there, but I couldn't. Just after I closed the window again, I heard Mollie scream and I rushed down.

TROTTER (*leaning on the refectory table*) Those simple actions took you rather a long time, didn't they, Mr Ralston?

GILES. I don't think so. (*He moves away to the stairs*)

TROTTER. I should say you definitely—took your time over them.

GILES. I was thinking about something.

TROTTER. Very well. Now then, Mr Wren, I'll have your account of where you were.

CHRISTOPHER (*rising and moving to* L *of Trotter*) I'd been in the kitchen, seeing if there was anything I could do to help Mrs Ralston. I adore cooking. After that I went upstairs to my bedroom.

TROTTER. Why?

CHRISTOPHER. It's quite a natural thing to go to one's

bedroom, don't you think? I mean—one does want to be alone *sometimes*.

TROTTER. You went to your bedroom because you wanted to be alone?

CHRISTOPHER. And I wanted to brush my hair—and—er—tidy up.

TROTTER (*looking hard at Christopher's dishevelled hair*) You wanted to brush your hair?

CHRISTOPHER. Anyway, that's where I was!

(GILES *moves down* L *to the door*)

TROTTER. And you heard Mrs Ralston scream?

CHRISTOPHER. Yes.

TROTTER. And you came down?

CHRISTOPHER. Yes.

TROTTER. Curious that you and Mr Ralston didn't meet on the stairs.

(CHRISTOPHER *and* GILES *look at each other*)

CHRISTOPHER. I came down by the back stairs. They're nearer to my room.

TROTTER. Did you go to your room by the back stairs, or did you come through here?

CHRISTOPHER. I went up by the back stairs, too. (*He moves to the desk chair and sits*)

TROTTER. I see. (*He moves to* R *of the sofa table*) Mr Paravicini?

PARAVICINI. I have told you. (*He rises and moves to* L *of the sofa*) I was playing the piano in the drawing-room—through there, Inspector. (*He gestures* L)

TROTTER. I'm not an Inspector—just a Sergeant, Mr Paravicini. Did anybody hear you playing the piano?

PARAVICINI (*smiling*) I do not expect so. I was playing very, very softly—with one finger—so.

MOLLIE. You were playing *Three Blind Mice*.

TROTTER (*sharply*) Is that so?

PARAVICINI. Yes. It is a very catchy little tune. It is—how shall I say?—a haunting little tune? Don't you all agree?

MOLLIE. I think it's horrible.

PARAVICINI. And yet—it runs in people's head. Someone was whistling it, too.

TROTTER. Whistling it? Where?

PARAVICINI. I am not sure. Perhaps in the front hall—perhaps on the stairs—perhaps even upstairs in a bedroom.

TROTTER. Who was whistling *Three Blind Mice*?

(*There is no answer*)

Are you making this up, Mr Paravicini?

PARAVICINI. No, no, Inspector—I beg your pardon—**Sergeant**, I would not do a thing like that.

TROTTER. Well, go on, you were playing the piano.

PARAVICINI (*holding out a finger*) With one finger—so . . . And then I hear the radio—playing very loud—someone is shouting on it. It offended my ears. And after that—suddenly—I hear Mrs Ralston scream. (*He sits at the L end of the sofa*)

TROTTER (*moving up to C of the refectory table; gesturing with his fingers*) Mr Ralston upstairs. Mr Wren upstairs. Mr Paravicini in drawing-room. Miss Casewell?

MISS CASEWELL. I was writing letters in the library.

TROTTER. Could you hear what was going on in here?

MISS CASEWELL. No, I didn't hear anything until Mrs Ralston screamed.

TROTTER. And what did you do then?

MISS CASEWELL. I came in here.

TROTTER. At once.

MISS CASEWELL. I—think so.

TROTTER. You say you were writing letters when you heard Mrs Ralston scream?

MISS CASEWELL. Yes.

TROTTER. And got up from the writing table hurriedly and came in here?

MISS CASEWELL. Yes.

TROTTER. And yet there doesn't seem to be any unfinished letter on the writing desk in the library.

MISS CASEWELL (*rising*) I brought it with me. (*She opens her handbag, takes out a letter, moves up to L of Trotter and hands it to him*)

TROTTER (*looking at it and handing it back*) Dearest Jessie—h'm —a friend of yours, or a relation?

MISS CASEWELL. That's none of your damned business. (*She turns away*)

TROTTER. Perhaps not. (*He moves round the R end of the refectory table to behind it C*) You know if I were to hear someone screaming blue murder when I was writing a letter, I don't believe I'd take the time to pick up my unfinished letter, fold it and put it in my handbag before going to see what was the matter.

MISS CASEWELL. You wouldn't? How interesting. (*She moves up the stairs and sits on the stool*)

TROTTER (*moving to L of Major Metcalf*) Now, Major Metcalf, what about you? You say you were in the cellar. Why?

MAJOR METCALF (*pleasantly*) Looking around. Just looking around. I looked into that cupboard place under the stairs near the kitchen. Lot of junk and sports tackle. And I noticed there was another door inside it, and I opened it and saw a flight of steps. I was curious and I went down. Nice cellars you've got.

MOLLIE. Glad you like them.

MAJOR METCALF. Not at all. Crypt of an old monastery, I should say. Probably why this place is called "Monkswell".

TROTTER. We're not engaged in antiquarian research, Major

Metcalf. We're investigating a murder. Mrs Ralston has told us that she heard a door shut with a faint creak. (*He moves to* R *of the sofa*) That particular door shuts with a creak. It could be, you know, that after killing Mrs Boyle, the murderer heard Mrs Ralston (*moving to* L *of the armchair* C) coming from the kitchen and slipped into the cupboard pulling the door to after him.

MAJOR METCALF. A lot of things could be.

(MOLLIE *rises, moves down to the small armchair and sits. There is a pause*)

CHRISTOPHER (*rising*) There would be fingerprints on the inside of the cupboard.

MAJOR METCALF. Mine are there all right. But most criminals are careful to wear gloves, aren't they?

TROTTER. It's usual. But all criminals slip up sooner or later.

PARAVICINI. I wonder, Sergeant, if that's really true?

GILES (*moving to* L *of Trotter*) Look here, aren't we wasting time? There's one person who . . .

TROTTER. Please, Mr Ralston, I'm in charge of this investigation.

GILES. Oh, very well, but . . .

(GILES *exits by the door down* L)

TROTTER (*calling authoritatively*) Mr Ralston!

(GILES *re-enters grudgingly and stands by the door*)

Thank you. (*Moving behind the refectory table*) We've got to establish opportunity, you know, as well as motive. And now let me tell you this—you *all* had opportunity.

(*There are several murmured protests*)

(*He holds up his hand*) There are two staircases—anyone could go up by one and come down by the other. Anyone could go down to the cellars by the door near the kitchen and come up by a flight of steps that leads up through a trap-door to the foot of the stairs over there. (*He points off* R) The vital fact was that every one of you was *alone* at the time the murder was committed.

GILES. But look here, Sergeant, you speak as though we were all under suspicion. That's absurd!

TROTTER. In a murder case, everyone is under suspicion.

GILES. But you know pretty well who killed that woman in Culver Street. You think it's the eldest of those three children at the farm. A mentally abnormal young man who is now twenty-three years of age. Well, damn it all, there's only one person here who fits the bill. (*He points to Christopher and moves slightly towards him*)

CHRISTOPHER. It's not true—it's not true! You're all against me. Everyone's always been against me. You're going to frame me for a murder. It's persecution, (*crossing to* L *of Major Metcalf*) that's what it is—persecution.

(GILES *follows him but pauses at the* L *end of the refectory table*)

MAJOR METCALF (*rising; kindly*) Steady, lad, steady. (*He pats Christopher on the shoulder, then he takes out his pipe*

MOLLIE (*rising and moving up to* L *of Christopher*) It's all right, Chris. Nobody's against you. (*To Trotter*) Tell him it's all right.

TROTTER (*looking at Giles; stolidly*) We don't frame people.

MOLLIE (*to Trotter*) Tell him you're not going to arrest him.

TROTTER (*moving to* L *of Mollie; stolidly*) I'm not arresting anyone. To do that, I've got to have evidence. I haven't got any evidence—yet.

(CHRISTOPHER *moves to the fire*)

GILES. I think you're crazy, Mollie. (*Moving up* C. *To Trotter*) And you, too! There's just one person who fits the bill and, if only as a safety measure, he ought to be put under arrest. It's only fair to the rest of us.

MOLLIE. Wait, Giles, wait. Sergeant Trotter, can I—can I speak to you a minute?

TROTTER. Certainly, Mrs Ralston. Will the rest of you go into the dining-room, please.

(*The others rise and move down* R *to the door: first* MISS CASEWELL, *then* MR PARAVICINI, *protesting, followed by* CHRISTOPHER *and* MAJOR METCALF, *who pauses to light his pipe.* MAJOR METCALF *becomes aware of being stared at. They all exit*)

GILES. I'm staying.

MOLLIE. No, Giles, you, too, please.

GILES (*furious*) I'm staying. I don't know what's come over you, Mollie.

MOLLIE. Please.

(GILES *exits after the others down* R, *leaving the door open.* MOLLIE *shuts it.* TROTTER *moves to the arch up* R)

TROTTER. Yes, Mrs Ralston, (*moving above the armchair* C) what is it you want to say to me?

MOLLIE (*moving up to* L *of Trotter*) Sergeant Trotter, you think that this—(*she moves below the sofa*) this crazy killer must be the —eldest of those three boys at the Farm—but you don't know that, do you?

TROTTER. We don't actually know a thing. All we've got so far is that the woman who joined with her husband in ill-treating and starving those children, has been killed, and that the woman magistrate who was responsible for placing them there has been killed. (*He moves down to* R *of the sofa*) The telephone wire that links me with police headquarters has been cut . . .

MOLLIE. You don't even know that. It may have been just the snow.

TROTTER. No, Mrs Ralston, the line was deliberately cut. It was cut just outside by the front door. I found the place.

MOLLIE (*shaken*) I see.

TROTTER. Sit down, Mrs Ralston.

MOLLIE (*sitting on the sofa*) But, all the same, you don't know . . .

TROTTER (*moving in a circle L above the sofa and then R below it*) I'm going by probability. It all points one way; mental instability, childish mentality, desertion from the Army and the psychiatrist's report.

MOLLIE. Oh I know, and therefore it all seems to point to Christopher. But I don't believe it is Christopher. There must be other possibilities.

TROTTER (R *of the sofa; turning to her*) Such as?

MOLLIE (*hesitating*) Well—hadn't those children any relations at all?

TROTTER. The mother was a drunk. She died soon after the children were taken away from her.

MOLLIE. What about their father?

TROTTER. He was an Army sergeant, serving abroad. If he's alive, he's probably discharged from the Army by now.

MOLLIE. You don't know where he is now?

TROTTER. We've no information. To trace him may take some time, but I can assure you, Mrs Ralston, that the police take every eventuality into account.

MOLLIE. But you don't know where he may be at this minute, and if the son is mentally unstable, the father may have been unstable, too.

TROTTER. Well, it's a possibility.

MOLLIE. If he came home, after being a prisoner with the Japs, perhaps, and having suffered terribly—if he came home and found his wife dead and that his children had gone through some terrible experience, and one of them had died through it, he might go off his head a bit and want—revenge!

TROTTER. That's only surmise.

MOLLIE. But it's possible?

TROTTER. Oh yes, Mrs Ralston, it's quite possible.

MOLLIE. So the murderer may be middle-aged, or even old. (*She pauses*) When I said the police had rung up, Major Metcalf was frightfully upset. He really was. I saw his face.

TROTTER (*considering*) Major Metcalf? (*He moves to the armchair* C *and sits*)

MOLLIE. Middle-aged. A soldier. He seems quite nice and perfectly normal—but it mightn't show, might it?

TROTTER. No, often it doesn't show at all.

MOLLIE (*rising and moving to* L *of Trotter*) So, it's not only Christopher who's a suspect. There's Major Metcalf as well.

TROTTER. Any other suggestions?

MOLLIE. Well, Mr Paravicini did drop the poker when I said the police had rung up.

TROTTER. Mr Paravicini. (*He appears to consider*)

MOLLIE. I know he seems quite old—and foreign and everything, but he mightn't really be as old as he looks. He moves like a much younger man, and he's definitely got make-up on his face. Miss Casewell noticed it, too. He might be—oh, I know it sounds very melodramatic—but he might be *disguised*.

TROTTER. You're very anxious, aren't you, that it shouldn't be young Mr Wren?

MOLLIE (*moving to the fire*) He seems so—helpless, somehow. (*Turning to Trotter*) And so unhappy.

TROTTER. Mrs Ralston, let me tell you something. I've had *all* possibilities in mind ever since the beginning. The boy Georgie, the father—and someone else. There was a sister, you remember.

MOLLIE. Oh—the sister?

TROTTER (*rising and moving to Mollie*) It could have been a woman who killed Maureen Lyon. A woman. (*Moving c*) The muffler pulled up and the man's felt hat pulled well down, and the killer whispered, you know. It's the voice that gives the sex away. (*He moves above the sofa table*) Yes, it might have been a woman.

MOLLIE. Miss Casewell?

TROTTER (*moving to the stairs*) She looks a bit old for the part. (*He moves up the stairs, opens the library door, looks in, then shuts the door*) Oh yes, Mrs Ralston, there's a very wide field. (*He comes down the stairs*) There's yourself, for instance.

MOLLIE. Me?

TROTTER. You're about the right age.

(MOLLIE *is about to protest*)

(*Checking her*) No, no. Whatever you tell me about yourself, I've got no means of checking it at this moment, remember. And then there's your husband.

MOLLIE. Giles, how ridiculous!

TROTTER (*crossing slowly to L of Mollie*) He and Christopher Wren are much of an age. Say, your husband looks older than his years, and Christopher Wren looks younger. Actual age is very hard to tell. How much do you know about your husband, Mrs Ralston?

MOLLIE. How much do I know about Giles? Oh, don't be silly.

TROTTER. You've been married—how long?

MOLLIE. Just a year.

TROTTER. And you met him—where?

MOLLIE. At a dance in London. We went in a party.

TROTTER. Did you meet his people?

MOLLIE. He hasn't any people. They're all dead.

TROTTER (*significantly*) They're all dead?

MOLLIE. Yes—but, oh you make it sound all wrong. His father was a barrister and his mother died when he was a baby.

TROTTER. You're only telling me what *he* told you.

MOLLIE. Yes—but . . . (*She turns away*)

TROTTER. You don't know it of your own knowledge.

MOLLIE (*turning back quickly*) It's outrageous that . . .

TROTTER. You'd be surprised, Mrs Ralston, if you knew how many cases rather like yours we get. Especially since the war. Homes broken up and families dead. Fellow says he's been in the Air Force, or just finished his Army training. Parents killed—no relations. There aren't any backgrounds nowadays and young people settle their own affairs—they meet and marry. It's parents and relatives who used to make the enquiries before they consented to an engagement. That's all done away with. Girl just marries her man. Sometimes she doesn't find out for a year or two that he's an absconding bank clerk, or an Army deserter or something equally undesirable. How long had you known Giles Ralston when you married him?

MOLLIE. Just three weeks. But . . .

TROTTER. And you don't know anything about him?

MOLLIE. That's not true. I know everything about him! I know exactly the sort of person he is. He's *Giles*. (*Turning to the fire*) And it's absolutely absurd to suggest that he's some horrible crazy homicidal maniac. Why, he wasn't even in London yesterday when the murder took place.

TROTTER. Where was he? Here?

MOLLIE. He went across country to a sale to get some wire netting for our chickens.

TROTTER. Bring it back with him? (*He crosses to the desk*)

MOLLIE. No, it turned out to be the wrong kind.

TROTTER. Only thirty miles from London, aren't you? Oh, you got an ABC? (*He picks up the ABC and reads it*) Only an hour by train—a little longer by car.

MOLLIE (*stamping her foot with temper*) I tell you Giles wasn't in London.

TROTTER. Just a minute, Mrs Ralston. (*He crosses to the front hall, and comes back carrying a darkish overcoat. Moving to L of Mollie*) This your husband's coat?

(MOLLIE *looks at the coat*)

MOLLIE (*suspiciously*) Yes.

(TROTTER *takes out a folded evening paper from the pocket*)

TROTTER. *Evening News.* Yesterday's. Sold on the streets about three-thirty yesterday afternoon.

MOLLIE. I don't believe it!

TROTTER. Don't you? (*He moves up* R *to the arch with the coat*)
Don't you?

(TROTTER *exits through the archway up* R *with the overcoat.*
MOLLIE *sits in the small armchair down* R, *staring at the evening
paper.*
  The door down R *slowly opens.* CHRISTOPHER *peeps in through
the door, sees that Mollie is alone and enters*)

CHRISTOPHER. Mollie!

(MOLLIE *jumps up and hides the newspaper under the cushion in
the armchair* C)

MOLLIE. Oh, you startled me! (*She moves* L *of the armchair* C)

CHRISTOPHER. Where is he? (*Moving to* R *of Mollie*) Where has
he gone?

MOLLIE. Who?

CHRISTOPHER. The sergeant.

MOLLIE. Oh, he went out that way.

CHRISTOPHER. If only I could get away. Somehow—some way.
Is there anywhere I could hide—in the house?

MOLLIE. Hide?

CHRISTOPHER. Yes—from *him*.

MOLLIE. Why?

CHRISTOPHER. But, darling, they're all so frightfully against
me. They're going to say I committed these murders—particularly your husband. (*He moves to* R *of the sofa*)

MOLLIE. Never mind him. (*She moves a step to* R *of Christopher*)
Listen, Christopher, you can't go on—running away from things
—all your life.

CHRISTOPHER. Why do you say that?

MOLLIE. Well, it's true, isn't it?

CHRISTOPHER (*hopelessly*) Oh yes, it's quite true. (*He sits at
the* L *end of the sofa*)

MOLLIE (*sitting at the* R *end of the sofa; affectionately*) You've got
to grow up some time, Chris.

CHRISTOPHER. I wish I hadn't.

MOLLIE. Your name isn't really Christopher Wren, is it?

CHRISTOPHER. No.

MOLLIE. And you're not really training to be an architect?

CHRISTOPHER. No.

MOLLIE. Why did you . . .?

CHRISTOPHER. Call myself Christopher Wren? It just amused
me. And then they used to laugh at me at school and call me
little Christopher Robin. Robin—Wren—association of ideas. It
was hell being at school.

MOLLIE. What's your real name?

CHRISTOPHER. We needn't go into that. I ran away whilst I was doing my Army service. It was all so beastly—I hated it.

(MOLLIE *has a sudden wave of unease, which* CHRISTOPHER *notices. She rises and moves to* R *of the sofa*)

(*Rising and moving down* L) Yes, I'm just like the unknown murderer.

(MOLLIE *moves up to* L *of the refectory table, and turns away from him*)

I told you I was the one the specification fitted. You see, my mother—my mother . . . (*He moves up to* L *of the sofa table*)

MOLLIE. Yes, your mother?

CHRISTOPHER. Everything would be all right if she hadn't died. She would have taken care of me—and looked after me . . .

MOLLIE. You can't go on being looked after all your life. Things happen to you. And you've got to bear them—you've got to go on just as usual.

CHRISTOPHER. One can't do that.

MOLLIE. Yes, one can.

CHRISTOPHER. You mean—you have? (*He moves up to* L *of Mollie*)

MOLLIE (*facing Christopher*) Yes.

CHRISTOPHER. What was it? Something very bad?

MOLLIE. Something I've never forgotten.

CHRISTOPHER. Was it to do with Giles?

MOLLIE. No, it was long before I met Giles.

CHRISTOPHER. You must have been very young. Almost a child.

MOLLIE. Perhaps that's why it was so—awful. It was horrible—horrible . . . I try to put it out of my mind. I try never to think about it.

CHRISTOPHER. So—you're running away, too. Running away from things—instead of facing them?

MOLLIE. Yes—perhaps, in a way, I am.

(*There is a silence*)

Considering that I never saw you until yesterday, we seem to know each other rather well.

CHRISTOPHER. Yes, it's odd, isn't it?

MOLLIE. I don't know. I suppose there's a sort of—sympathy between us.

CHRISTOPHER. Anyway, you think I ought to stick it out.

MOLLIE. Well, frankly, what else can you do?

CHRISTOPHER. I might pinch the sergeant's skis. I can ski quite well.

MOLLIE. That would be frightfully stupid. It would be almost like admitting you're guilty.

CHRISTOPHER. Sergeant Trotter thinks I'm guilty.

MOLLIE. No, he doesn't. At least—I don't know what he thinks. (*She moves down to the armchair* C, *pulls out the evening paper from under the cushion and stares at it. Suddenly, with passion*) I hate him—I hate him—I hate him . . .

CHRISTOPHER (*startled*) Who?

MOLLIE. Sergeant Trotter. He puts things into your head. Things that aren't true, that can't possibly be true.

CHRISTOPHER. What is all this?

MOLLIE. I don't believe it—I won't believe it . . .

CHRISTOPHER. What won't you believe? (*He moves slowly to Mollie, puts his hands on her shoulders and turns her round to face him*) Come on—out with it!

MOLLIE (*showing the paper*) You see that?

CHRISTOPHER. Yes.

MOLLIE. What is it? Yesterday's evening paper—a London paper. And it was in Giles' pocket. But Giles didn't go to London yesterday.

CHRISTOPHER. Well, if he was here all day . . .

MOLLIE. But he wasn't. He went off in the car to look for chicken wire, but he couldn't find any.

CHRISTOPHER. Well, that's all right. (*Moving* LC) Probably he did go up to London after all.

MOLLIE. Then why shouldn't he tell me he did? Why pretend he'd been driving all round the countryside?

CHRISTOPHER. Perhaps, with the news of this murder . . .

MOLLIE. He didn't know about the murder. Or did he? Did he? (*She moves to the fire*)

CHRISTOPHER. Good Lord, Mollie. Surely you don't think— the Sergeant doesn't think . . .

(*During the next speech* MOLLIE *crosses slowly up stage to* L *of the sofa.* CHRISTOPHER *silently drops the paper on the sofa*)

MOLLIE. I don't know what the Sergeant thinks. And he can make you think things about people. You ask yourself questions and you begin to doubt. You feel that somebody you love and know well might be—a stranger. (*Whispering*) That's what happens in a nightmare. You're somewhere in the middle of friends and then you suddenly look at their faces and they're not your friends any longer—they're different people—just pretending. Perhaps you can't trust anybody—perhaps everybody's a stranger. (*She puts her hands to her face*)

(CHRISTOPHER *moves to the* L *end of the sofa, kneels on it and takes her hands away from her face.*

GILES *enters from the dining-room down* R, *but stops when he sees them.* MOLLIE *backs away, and* CHRISTOPHER *sits on the sofa*)

GILES (*at the door*) I seem to be interrupting something.

D

MOLLIE. No, we were—just talking. I must go to the kitchen—there's the pie and potatoes—and I must do—do the spinach. (*She moves* R *above the armchair* C)

CHRISTOPHER (*rising and moving* C) I'll come and give you a hand.

GILES (*moving up to the fire*) No, you won't.

MOLLIE. Giles.

GILES. *Tête-à-têtes* aren't very healthy things at present. You keep out of the kitchen and keep away from my wife.

CHRISTOPHER. But really, look here . . .

GILES (*furious*) You keep away from my wife, Wren. She's not going to be the next victim.

CHRISTOPHER. So that's what you think about me.

GILES. I've already said so, haven't I? There's a killer loose in this house—and it seems to me you fit the bill.

CHRISTOPHER. I'm not the only one to fit the bill.

GILES. I don't see who else does.

CHRISTOPHER. How blind you are—or do you just pretend to be blind?

GILES. I tell you I'm worrying about my wife's safety.

CHRISTOPHER. So am I. I'm not going to leave you here alone with her. (*He moves up to* L *of Mollie*)

GILES (*moving up to* R *of Mollie*) What the hell . . .?

MOLLIE. Please go, Chris.

CHRISTOPHER. I'm not going.

MOLLIE. Please go, Christopher. Please. I mean it . . .

CHRISTOPHER (*moving* R) I shan't be far away.

(*Unwillingly* CHRISTOPHER *exits through the arch up* R. MOLLIE *crosses to the desk chair, and* GILES *follows her*)

GILES. What is all this? Mollie, you must be crazy. Perfectly prepared to shut yourself up in the kitchen with a homicidal maniac.

MOLLIE. He isn't.

GILES. You've only got to look at him to see he's barmy.

MOLLIE. He isn't. He's just unhappy. I tell you, Giles, he isn't dangerous. I'd know if he was dangerous. And anyway, I can look after myself.

GILES. That's what Mrs Boyle said!

MOLLIE. Oh, Giles—don't. (*She moves down* L)

GILES (*moving down to* R *of Mollie*) Look here, what is there between you and that wretched boy?

MOLLIE. What do you mean by between us? I'm sorry for him—that's all.

GILES. Perhaps you'd met him before. Perhaps you suggested to him to come here and that you'd both pretend to meet for the first time. All cooked up between you, was it?

MOLLIE. Giles, have you gone out of your mind? How dare you suggest these things?

GILES (*moving up to* C *of the refectory table*) Rather odd, isn't it, that he should come and stay at an out-of-the-way place like this?

MOLLIE. No odder than that Miss Casewell and Major Metcalf and Mrs Boyle should.

GILES. I read once in a paper that these homicidal cases were able to attract women. Looks as though it were true. (*He moves down* C) Where did you first know him? How long has this been going on?

MOLLIE. You're being absolutely ridiculous. (*She moves* R *slightly*) I never set eyes on Christopher Wren until he arrived yesterday.

GILES. That's what you say. Perhaps you've been running up to London to meet him on the sly.

MOLLIE. You know perfectly well that I haven't been up to London for weeks.

GILES (*in a peculiar tone*) You haven't been up to London for weeks. Is—that—so?

MOLLIE. What on earth do you mean? It's quite true.

GILES. Is it? Then what's this? (*He takes out Mollie's glove from his pocket and draws out of it the bus ticket*)

     (MOLLIE *starts*)

This is one of the gloves you were wearing yesterday. You dropped it. I picked it up this afternoon when I was talking to Sergeant Trotter. You see what's inside—a London bus ticket!

MOLLIE (*looking guilty*) Oh—that . . .

GILES (*turning away* RC) So it seems that you didn't only go to the village yesterday, you went to London as well.

MOLLIE. All right, I went to . . .

GILES. Whilst I was safely away racing round the countryside.

MOLLIE (*with emphasis*) Whilst you were racing round the countryside . . .

GILES. Come on now—admit it. You went to London.

MOLLIE. All right. (*She moves* C *below the sofa*) I went to London. So did you!

GILES. What?

MOLLIE. So did you. You brought back an evening paper. (*She picks up the paper from the sofa*)

GILES. Where did you get hold of that?

MOLLIE. It was in your overcoat pocket.

GILES. Anyone could have put it in there.

MOLLIE. Did they? No, you were in London.

GILES. All right. Yes, I was in London. I didn't go to meet a woman there.

MOLLIE (*in horror; whispering*) Didn't you—are you sure you didn't?

GILES. Eh? What d'you mean? (*He comes nearer to her*)

(Mollie *recoils, backing away down* L)

Mollie. Go away. Don't come near me.
Giles (*following her*) What's the matter?
Mollie. Don't touch me.
Giles. Did you go to London yesterday to meet Christopher Wren?
Mollie. Don't be a fool. Of course I didn't.
Giles. Then why did you go?

(Mollie *changes her manner. She smiles in a dreamy fashion*)

Mollie. I—shan't tell you that. Perhaps—now—I've forgotten why I went . . . (*She crosses towards the archway up* R)
Giles (*moving to* L *of Mollie*) Mollie, what's come over you? You're different all of a sudden. I feel as though I don't know you any more.
Mollie. Perhaps you never did know me. We've been married how long—a year? But you don't really know anything about me. What I'd done or thought or felt or suffered before you knew me.
Giles. Mollie, you're crazy . . .
Mollie. All right then, I'm crazy! Why not? Perhaps it's fun to be crazy!
Giles (*angrily*) What the hell are you . . .?

(Mr Paravicini *enters from the archway up* R. *He moves between them*)

Paravicini. Now, now. I do hope you young people are not both saying a little more than you mean. One is so apt to in these lovers' quarrels.
Giles. "Lovers' quarrels"! That's good. (*He moves to* L *of the refectory table*)
Paravicini (*moving down to the small armchair* R) Quite so. Quite so. I know just how you feel. I have been through all this myself when I was a younger man. *Jeunesse—jeunesse*—as the poet says. Not been married long, I imagine?
Giles (*crossing to the fire*) It's no business of yours, Mr Paravicini . . .
Paravicini (*moving down* C) No, no, no business at all. But I just came in to say that the Sergeant cannot find his skis and I'm afraid he is very annoyed.
Mollie (*moving to* R *of the sofa table*) Christopher!
Giles. What's that?
Paravicini (*moving to face Giles*) He wants to know if you have by any chance moved them, Mr Ralston.
Giles. No, of course not.

(Sergeant Trotter *enters from the archway up* R *looking red and annoyed*)

TROTTER. Mr Ralston—Mrs Ralston, have you removed my skis from the cupboard back there where we put them?

GILES. Certainly not.

TROTTER. Somebody's taken them.

PARAVICINI (*moving to* R *of Trotter*) What made you happen to look for them?

TROTTER. The snow is still lying. I need help here, reinforcements. I was going to ski over to the police station at Market Hampton to report on the situation.

PARAVICINI. And now you can't—dear, dear . . . Somebody's seen to it that you certainly shan't do that. But there could be another reason, couldn't there?

TROTTER. Yes, what?

PARAVICINI. Somebody may want to get away.

GILES (*moving to* R *of Mollie; to her*) What did you mean when you said "Christopher" just now?

MOLLIE. Nothing.

PARAVICINI (*chuckling*) So our young architect has hooked it, has he? Very, very interesting.

TROTTER. Is this true, Mrs Ralston? (*He moves to* C *of the refectory table*)

(CHRISTOPHER *enters from the stairs* L *and comes to* L *of the sofa*)

MOLLIE (*moving slightly* L) Oh, thank goodness. You haven't gone, after all.

TROTTER (*crossing to* R *of Christopher*) Did you take my skis, Mr Wren?

CHRISTOPHER (*surprised*) Your skis, Sergeant? No, why should I?

TROTTER. Mrs Ralston seemed to think . . . (*He looks at Mollie*)

MOLLIE. Mr Wren is very fond of ski-ing. I thought he might have taken them just to—get a little exercise.

GILES. Exercise? (*He moves up to* C *of the refectory table*)

TROTTER. Now, listen, you people. This is a serious matter. Somebody has removed my only chance of communication with the outside world. I want everybody here—at once.

PARAVICINI. I think Miss Casewell has gone upstairs.

MOLLIE. I'll get her.

(MOLLIE *exits up the stairs.* TROTTER *moves to* L *of the arch up* L)

PARAVICINI (*moving down* R) I left Major Metcalf in the dining-room. (*He opens the door down* R *and looks in*) Major Metcalf! He's not there now.

GILES. I'll try and find him.

(GILES *exits up* R.

MOLLIE *and* MISS CASEWELL *enter from the stairs.* MOLLIE *moves to* R *of the refectory table and* MISS CASEWELL *to* L *of it.*

MAJOR METCALF *enters up* L *from the library*)

MAJOR METCALF. Hullo, wanting me?

TROTTER. It's a question of my skis.

MAJOR METCALF. Skis? (*He moves to* L *of the sofa*)

PARAVICINI (*moving to the archway up* R *and calling*)   Mr Ralston!

(GILES *enters up* R *and stands below the arch.* PARAVICINI *returns and sits in the small armchair down* R)

TROTTER. Did either of you two remove a pair of skis from the cupboard near the kitchen door?

MISS CASEWELL. Good Lord, no. Why should I?

MAJOR METCALF. And *I* didn't touch 'em.

TROTTER. Nevertheless they are gone. (*To Miss Casewell*) Which way did you go to your room?

MISS CASEWELL. By the back stairs.

TROTTER. Then you passed the cupboard door.

MISS CASEWELL. If you say so—I've no idea where your skis are.

TROTTER (*to Major Metcalf*) You were actually *in* that cupboard today.

MAJOR METCALF. Yes, I was.

TROTTER. At the time Mrs Boyle was killed.

MAJOR METCALF. At the time Mrs Boyle was killed I'd gone down to the cellar.

TROTTER. Were the skis in the cupboard when you passed through?

MAJOR METCALF. I haven't the least idea.

TROTTER. Didn't you see them there?

MAJOR METCALF. Can't remember.

TROTTER. You must remember if those skis were there then?

MAJOR METCALF. No good shouting at me, young fellow. I wasn't thinking about any damned skis. I was interested in the cellars. (*He moves to the sofa and sits*) Architecture of this place is very interesting. I opened the other door and I went on down. So I can't tell you whether the skis were there or not.

TROTTER (*moving down to* L *of the sofa*) You realize that you, yourself, had an excellent opportunity of taking them?

MAJOR METCALF. Yes, yes, I grant you that. If I wanted to, that is.

TROTTER. The question is, where are they now?

MAJOR METCALF. Ought to be able to find them if we all set to. Not a case of "Hunt the Thimble". Whacking great things, skis. Supposing we all set to. (*He rises and crosses* R *towards the door*)

TROTTER. Not quite so fast, Major Metcalf. That may be, you know, what we are meant to do.

MAJOR METCALF. Eh, I don't get you?

TROTTER. I'm in the position now where I've got to put myself in the place of a crazy cunning brain. I've got to ask myself what he wants us to do and what he, himself, is planning to do next.

I've got to try and keep just one step ahead of him. Because, if I don't, there's going to be another death.

Miss Casewell. You still don't believe that?

Trotter. Yes, Miss Casewell. I do. Three blind mice. Two mice cancelled out—a third mouse still to be dealt with. (*Moving down* C, *with his back to the audience*) There are six of you here listening to me. One of you's a killer!

(*There is a pause. They are all affected and look uneasily at one another*)

One of you's a killer. (*He moves to the fire*) I don't know which yet, but I shall. And another of you is the killer's prospective victim. That's the person I'm speaking to. (*He crosses to Mollie*) Mrs Boyle held out on me—Mrs Boyle is dead. (*He moves up* C) You—whoever you are—are holding out on me. Well—don't. Because you're in danger. Nobody who's killed twice is going to hesitate to kill a third time. (*He moves to* R *of Major Metcalf*) And as it is, I don't know which of you it is who needs protection.

(*There is a pause*)

(*Crossing down* C *and turning his back to the audience*) Come on, now, anybody here who has anything, however slight, to reproach themselves for in that bygone business, had better come out with it.

(*There is a pause*)

All right—you won't. I'll get the killer—I've no doubt of that —but it may be too late for one of you. (*He moves up to* C *of the refectory table*) And I'll tell you another thing. The killer's enjoying this. Yes, he's enjoying himself a good deal . . .

(*There is a pause*)

(*He moves round the* R *end of the refectory table to behind it. He opens the* R *curtain, looks out and then sits at the* R *end of the window seat*) All right—you can go.

(Major Metcalf *exits into the dining-room down* R.

Christopher *exits up the stairs* L. Miss Casewell *crosses to the fire and leans on the mantelpiece.* Giles *moves* C *and* Mollie *follows;* Giles *stops and turns* R. Mollie *turns her back on him and moves behind the armchair* C. Paravicini *rises and moves to* R *of Mollie*)

Paravicini. Talking of chicken, dear lady, have you ever tried chicken's livers served on toast that has been thickly smeared with *foie gras*, with a very thin rasher of bacon just touched with a *soupçon* of fresh mustard? I will come with you to the kitchen and we will see what we can concoct together. A charming occupation.

(Paravicini *takes Mollie's right arm and starts to move up* R)

GILES (*taking Mollie's left arm*)   I'm helping my wife, Paravicini.

(MOLLIE *throws off Giles' arm*)

PARAVICINI. Your husband is afraid for you. Quite natural under the circumstances. He doesn't fancy your being alone with me.

(MOLLIE *throws off Paravicini's arm*)

It is my sadistic tendencies he fears—not my dishonourable ones. (*He leers*) Alas, what an inconvenience the husband always is. (*He kisses her fingers*) A riverderla . . .

MOLLIE. I'm sure Giles doesn't think . . .

PARAVICINI. He is very wise. Take no chances. (*He moves down to R of the armchair C*) Can I prove to you or to him or to our dogged Sergeant that I am *not* a homicidal maniac? So difficult to prove a negative. And suppose that instead I am really . . . (*He hums the tune of "Three Blind Mice"*)

MOLLIE. Oh don't. (*She moves to the back of the armchair C*)

PARAVICINI. But such a gay little tune? Don't you think? She cut off their tails with a carving knife—snick, snick, snick—delicious. Just what a child would adore. Cruel little things, children. (*Leaning forward*) Some of them never grow up.

(MOLLIE *gives a frightened cry*)

GILES (*moving to R of the refectory table*)   Stop frightening my wife at once.

MOLLIE. It's silly of me. But you see—I found her. Her face was all purple. I can't forget it . . .

PARAVICINI. I know. It's difficult to forget things, isn't it. You aren't really the forgetting kind.

MOLLIE (*incoherently*)   I must go—the food—dinner—prepare the spinach—and the potatoes all going to pieces—please, Giles.

(GILES *and* MOLLIE *exit through the archway up* R. PARAVICINI *leans on the* L *side of the arch and looks after them, grinning.* MISS CASEWELL *stands by the fireplace, lost in thought*)

TROTTER (*rising and crossing to* L *of Paravicini*)   What did you say to the lady to upset her, sir?

PARAVICINI. Me, Sergeant? Oh, just a little innocent fun. I've always been fond of a little joke.

TROTTER. There's nice fun—and there's fun that's not so nice.

PARAVICINI (*moving down* C)   Now I do wonder what you mean by that, Sergeant?

TROTTER. I've been doing a little wondering about you, sir.

PARAVICINI. Indeed?

TROTTER. I've been wondering about that car of yours, and how it happened to overturn in a snowdrift (*he pauses and draws the* R *curtain*) so conveniently.

PARAVICINI. Inconveniently, you mean, don't you, Sergeant?

TROTTER (*moving down to* R *of Paravicini*) That rather depends on the way you're looking at it. Just where were you bound for, by the way, when you had this—accident?

PARAVICINI. Oh—I was on my way to see a friend.

TROTTER. In this neighbourhood?

PARAVICINI. Not so very far from here.

TROTTER. And what was the name and address of this friend?

PARAVICINI. Now really, Sergeant Trotter, does that matter now? I mean, it has nothing to do with this predicament, has it? (*He sits at the* L *end of the sofa*)

TROTTER. We always like the fullest information. What did you say this friend's name was?

PARAVICINI. I didn't say. (*He takes a cigar from a case in his pocket*)

TROTTER. No, you didn't say. And it seems you're not going to say. (*He sits on the right arm of the sofa*) Now that's very interesting.

PARAVICINI. But there might be—so many reasons. An *amour* —discretion. These jealous husbands. (*He pierces the cigar*)

TROTTER. Rather old to be running round with the ladies at your time of life, aren't you?

PARAVICINI. My dear Sergeant, I am not, perhaps, quite so old as I look.

TROTTER. That's just what I've been thinking, sir.

PARAVICINI. What? (*He lights the cigar*)

TROTTER. That you may not be as old as you—try to look. There's a lot of people trying to look younger than they are. If somebody goes about trying to look older—well, it does make one ask oneself why.

PARAVICINI. Having asked questions of so many people—you ask questions of yourself as well? Isn't that overdoing things?

TROTTER. I might get an answer from myself—I don't get many from you.

PARAVICINI. Well, well—try again—that is, if you have any more questions to ask.

TROTTER. One or two. Where were you coming from last night?

PARAVICINI. That is simple—from London.

TROTTER. What address in London?

PARAVICINI. I always stay at the Ritz Hotel.

TROTTER. Very nice, too, I'm sure. What is your permanent address?

PARAVICINI. I dislike permanency.

TROTTER. What's your business or profession?

PARAVICINI. I play the markets.

TROTTER. Stockbroker?

PARAVICINI. No, no, you misunderstand me.

TROTTER. Enjoying this little game, aren't you? Sure of yourself, too. But I shouldn't be too sure. You're mixed up in a murder case, and don't you forget it. Murder isn't just fun and games.

PARAVICINI. Not even this murder? (*He gives a little giggle, and looks sideways at Trotter*) Dear me, you're very serious, Sergeant Trotter. I always have thought policemen have no sense of humour. (*He rises and moves to L of the sofa*) Is the inquisition over —for the moment?

TROTTER. For the moment—yes.

PARAVICINI. Thank you so much. I shall go and look for your skis in the drawing-room. Just in case someone has hidden them in the grand piano.

(*PARAVICINI exits down L. TROTTER looks after him, frowning, moves down to the door and opens it. MISS CASEWELL crosses quietly towards the stairs L. TROTTER shuts the door*)

TROTTER (*without turning his head*) Just a minute, please.

MISS CASEWELL (*pausing at the stairs*) Were you speaking to me?

TROTTER. Yes. (*Crossing to the armchair C*) Perhaps you'd come and sit down. (*He arranges the armchair for her*)

(*MISS CASEWELL looks at him warily and crosses below the sofa*)

MISS CASEWELL. Well, what do you want?

TROTTER. You may have heard some of the questions I was asking Mr Paravicini?

MISS CASEWELL. I heard them.

TROTTER (*moving to the R end of the sofa*) I'd like to have a little information from you.

MISS CASEWELL (*moving to the armchair C and sitting*) What do you want to know?

TROTTER. Full name, please.

MISS CASEWELL. Leslie Margaret (*she pauses*) Katherine Casewell.

TROTTER (*with just a nuance of something different*) Katherine . . .

MISS CASEWELL. I spell it with a "K".

TROTTER. Quite so. Address?

MISS CASEWELL. Villa Mariposa, Pine d'or, Majorca.

TROTTER. That's in Italy?

MISS CASEWELL. It's an island—a Spanish island.

TROTTER. I see. And your address in England?

MISS CASEWELL. Care of Morgan's Bank, Leadenhall Street.

TROTTER. No other English address?

MISS CASEWELL. No.

TROTTER. How long have you been in England?

MISS CASEWELL. A week.

TROTTER. And you have been staying since your arrival . . .?

MISS CASEWELL. At the Ledbury Hotel, Knightsbridge.

TROTTER (*sitting at the* R *end of the sofa*)   What brought you to Monkswell Manor, Miss Casewell?

MISS CASEWELL. I wanted somewhere quiet—in the country.

TROTTER. How long did you—or do you—propose to remain here? (*He starts twirling his hair with his right hand*)

MISS CASEWELL. Until I have finished what I came here to do. (*She notices the twirling*)

(TROTTER *looks up startled by a force in her words. She stares at him*)

TROTTER. And what was that?

(*There is a pause*)

And what was that? (*He stops twirling his hair*)

MISS CASEWELL (*with a puzzled frown*) Eh?

TROTTER. What was it you came here to do?

MISS CASEWELL. I beg your pardon. I was thinking of something else.

TROTTER (*rising and moving to* L *of Miss Casewell*) You haven't answered my question.

MISS CASEWELL. I really don't see, you know, why I should. It's a matter that concerns me alone. A strictly private affair.

TROTTER. All the same, Miss Casewell . . .

MISS CASEWELL (*rising and moving to the fire*) No, I don't think we'll argue about it.

TROTTER (*following her*) Would you mind telling me your age?

MISS CASEWELL. Not in the least. It's on my passport. I am twenty-four.

TROTTER. Twenty-four?

MISS CASEWELL. You were thinking I look older. That is quite true.

TROTTER. Is there anyone in this country who can—vouch for you?

MISS CASEWELL. My bank will reassure you as to my financial position. I can also refer you to a solicitor—a very discreet man. I am not in a position to offer you a social reference. I have lived most of my life abroad.

TROTTER. In Majorca?

MISS CASEWELL. In Majorca—and other places.

TROTTER. Were you born abroad?

MISS CASEWELL. No, I left England when I was thirteen.

(*There is a pause, with a feeling of tension in it*)

TROTTER. You know, Miss Casewell, I can't quite make you out. (*He backs away* L *slightly*)

MISS CASEWELL. Does it matter?

TROTTER. I don't know. (*He sits in the armchair* C) What are you doing here?

MISS CASEWELL. It seems to worry you.

TROTTER. It does worry me . . . (*He stares at her*) You went abroad when you were thirteen?

MISS CASEWELL. Twelve—thirteen—thereabouts.

TROTTER. Was your name Casewell then?

MISS CASEWELL. It's my name now.

TROTTER. What was your name then? Come on—tell me.

MISS CASEWELL. What are you trying to prove? (*She loses her calm*)

TROTTER. I want to know what your name was when you left England?

MISS CASEWELL. It's a long time ago. I've forgotten.

TROTTER. There are things one doesn't forget.

MISS CASEWELL. Possibly.

TROTTER. Unhappiness—despair . . .

MISS CASEWELL. I daresay . . .

TROTTER. What's your real name?

MISS CASEWELL. I told you—Leslie Margaret Katherine Casewell. (*She sits in the small armchair down* R)

TROTTER (*rising*) Katherine . . .? (*He stands over her*) What the hell are you doing here?

MISS CASEWELL. I . . . Oh God . . . (*She rises, moves* C, *and drops on the sofa. She cries, rocking herself to and fro*) I wish to God I'd never come here.

(TROTTER, *startled, moves to* R *of the sofa.* CHRISTOPHER *enters from the door down* L)

CHRISTOPHER (*coming to* L *of the sofa*) I always thought the police weren't allowed to give people the third degree.

TROTTER. I have merely been interrogating Miss Casewell.

CHRISTOPHER. You seem to have upset her. (*To Miss Casewell*) What did he do?

MISS CASEWELL. No, it's nothing. It's just—all this—murder—it's so horrible. (*She rises and faces Trotter*) It came over me suddenly. I'll go up to my room.

(MISS CASEWELL *exits up the stairs* L)

TROTTER (*moving to the stairs and looking up after her*) It's impossible . . . I can't believe it . . .

CHRISTOPHER (*moving up and leaning over the desk chair*) What can't you believe? Six impossible things before breakfast like the Red Queen.

TROTTER. Oh yes. It's rather like that.

CHRISTOPHER. Dear me—you look as though you'd seen a ghost.

TROTTER (*resuming his usual manner*) I've seen something I ought to have seen before. (*He moves* C) Blind as a bat, I've been. But I think now we may be able to get somewhere.

CHRISTOPHER (*impertinently*) The police have a clue.

TROTTER (*moving* R *of the sofa table; with a hint of menace*) Yes, Mr Wren—at last the police *have* a clue. I want everyone assembled in here again. Do you know where they are?

CHRISTOPHER (*moving to* L *of Trotter*) Giles and Mollie are in the kitchen. I have been helping Major Metcalf to look for your skis. We've looked in the most entertaining places—but all to no avail. I don't know where Paravicini is.

TROTTER. I'll get him. (*He moves down* L *to the door*) You get the others.

(CHRISTOPHER *exits up* R)

(*Opening the door*) Mr Paravicini. (*Moving below the sofa*) Mr Paravicini. (*Returning to the door and shouting*) Paravicini! (*He moves up to* C *of the refectory table*)

(PARAVICINI *enters gaily down* L)

PARAVICINI. Yes, Sergeant? (*He moves to the desk chair*) What can I do for you? Little Bo Policeman has lost his skis and doesn't know where to find them. Leave them alone, and they'll come home, dragging a murderer behind them. (*He moves down* L)

(MAJOR METCALF *enters through the arch up* R. GILES *and* MOLLIE *enter up* R, *with* CHRISTOPHER)

MAJOR METCALF. What is all this? (*He moves down to the fire*)

TROTTER. Sit down, Major, Mrs Ralston . . .

(*No-one sits.* MOLLIE *moves above the armchair* C, GILES *moves to* R *of the refectory table and* CHRISTOPHER *stands between them*)

MOLLIE. *Must* I come now? It's very inconvenient.

TROTTER. There are more important things than meals, Mrs Ralston. Mrs Boyle, for instance, won't want another meal.

MAJOR METCALF. That's a very tactless way of putting things, Sergeant.

TROTTER. I'm sorry, but I want co-operation and I intend to get it. Mr Ralston, will you go and ask Miss Casewell to come down again? She went up in her room. Tell her it will only be for a few minutes.

(GILES *exits to the stairs* L)

MOLLIE (*moving to* R *of the refectory table*) Have your skis been found, Sergeant?

TROTTER. No, Mrs Ralston, but I may say I have a very shrewd suspicion of who took them, and of why they were taken. I won't say any more at the present moment.

PARAVICINI. Please don't. (*He moves up to the desk chair*) I always think explanations should be kept to the very end. That exciting last chapter, you know.

TROTTER (*reprovingly*) This isn't a game, sir.

CHRISTOPHER. Isn't it? Now there I think you are wrong. I think it *is* a game—to somebody.

PARAVICINI. You think the murderer is enjoying himself. Maybe—maybe. (*He sits in the desk chair*)

(GILES *and* MISS CASEWELL, *now quite composed, enter from the stairs* L)

MISS CASEWELL. What is happening?

TROTTER. Sit down, Miss Casewell, Mrs Ralston . . .

(MISS CASEWELL *sits on the right arm of the sofa*, MOLLIE *moves down and sits in the armchair* C. GILES *remains standing at the bottom of the stairs*)

(*Officially*) Will you all pay attention, please? (*He sits* C *on the refectory table*) You may remember that after the murder of Mrs Boyle, I took statements from you all. Those statements related to your positions at the time the murder was committed. These statements were as follows: (*he consults his notebook*) Mrs Ralston in the kitchen, Mr Paravicini playing the piano in the drawing-room, Mr Ralston in his bedroom. Mr Wren ditto. Miss Casewell in the library. Major Metcalf (*he pauses and looks at Major Metcalf*) in the cellar.

MAJOR METCALF. Correct.

TROTTER. Those were the statements you made. I had no means of checking these statements. They may be true—they may not. To put it quite clearly, five of those statements are true, but one is false—which one? (*He pauses while he looks from one to the other*) Five of you were speaking the truth, one of you was lying. I have a plan that may help me to discover the liar. And if I discover that one of you lied to me—then I know who the murderer is.

MISS CASEWELL. Not necessarily. Someone may have lied—for some other reason.

TROTTER. I rather doubt that.

GILES. But what's the idea? You've just said you had no means of checking these statements.

TROTTER. No, but supposing everyone was to go through these actions a second time.

PARAVICINI (*sighing*) Ah, that old chestnut. Reconstruction of the crime.

GILES. That's a foreign idea.

TROTTER. Not a reconstruction of the *crime*, Mr Paravicini. A reconstruction of the movements of apparently innocent persons.

MAJOR METCALF. And what do you expect to learn from that?

TROTTER. You will forgive me if I don't make that clear just at the moment.

GILES. You want—a repeat performance?

TROTTER. Yes, Mr Ralston, I do.

MOLLIE. It's a trap.

TROTTER. What do you mean, it's a trap?

MOLLIE. It is a trap. I know it is.

TROTTER. I only want people to do exactly what they did before.

CHRISTOPHER (*also suspicious*) But I don't see—I simply can't see—what you can possibly hope to find out by just making people do the things they did before. I think it's just nonsense.

TROTTER. Do you, Mr Wren?

MOLLIE. Well, you can count me out. I'm too busy in the kitchen. (*She rises and moves up* R)

TROTTER. I can't count anybody out. (*He rises and looks round at them*) One might almost believe that you're *all* guilty by the looks of you. Why are you all so unwilling?

GILES. Of course, what you say goes, Sergeant. We'll all co-operate. Eh, Mollie?

MOLLIE (*unwilling*) Very well.

GILES. Wren?

(CHRISTOPHER *nods*)

Miss Casewell?

MISS CASEWELL. Yes.

GILES. Paravicini?

PARAVICINI (*throwing up his hands*) Oh yes, I consent.

GILES. Metcalf?

MAJOR METCALF (*slowly*) Yes.

GILES. Are we all to do exactly what we did before?

TROTTER. The same actions will be performed, yes.

PARAVICINI (*rising*) Then I will return to the piano in the drawing-room. Once again I will pick out with one finger the signature tune of a murderer. (*He sings, gesturing with his finger*) Tum, dum, dum—dum dum dum . . . (*He moves down* L)

TROTTER (*moving down* C) Not quite so fast, Mr Paravicini. (*To Mollie*) Do you play the piano, Mrs Ralston?

MOLLIE. Yes, I do.

TROTTER. And you know the tune of *Three Blind Mice*?

MOLLIE. Don't we all know it?

TROTTER. Then you could pick it out on the piano with one finger just as Mr Paravicini did.

(MOLLIE *nods*)

Good. Please go into the drawing-room, sit at the piano, and be ready to play when I give you the signal.

(MOLLIE *crosses* L *below the sofa*)

PARAVICINI. But, Sergeant, I understood that we were each to repeat our former roles.

TROTTER. The same actions will be performed, *but not necessarily by the same people*. Thank you, Mrs Ralston.

(PARAVICINI *opens the door down* L.
MOLLIE *exits*)

GILES. I don't see the point.

TROTTER (*moving up to* C *of the refectory table*) There is a point. It is a means of checking up on the original statements, and maybe *one* statement in particular. Now then, will you all pay attention, please. I will assign each of you your new stations. Mr Wren, will you kindly go to the kitchen. Just keep an eye on Mrs Ralston's dinner for her. You're very fond of cooking, I believe.

(CHRISTOPHER *exits up* R)

Mr Paravicini, will you go up to Mr Wren's room. By the back stairs is the most convenient way. Major Metcalf, will you go up to Mr Ralston's room and examine the telephone there. Miss Casewell, would you mind going down to the cellars? Mr Wren will show you the way. Unfortunately, I need someone to reproduce my own actions. I am sorry to ask it of you, Mr Ralston, but would you go out by that window and follow the telephone wire round to near the front door. Rather a chilly job—but you're probably the toughest person here.

MAJOR METCALF. And what are you going to do?

TROTTER (*crossing to the radio and switching it on and off*) I am enacting the part of Mrs Boyle.

MAJOR METCALF. Taking a bit of a risk, aren't you?

TROTTER (*reeling against the desk*) You will all stay in your places and remain there until you hear me call you.

(MISS CASEWELL *rises and exits up* R. GILES *moves behind the refectory table and opens the* R *curtain.*

MAJOR METCALF *exits up* L. TROTTER *nods to Paravicini to leave*)

PARAVICINI (*shrugging his shoulders*) Parlour games!

(PARAVICINI *exits up* R)

GILES. No objection to my wearing a coat?

TROTTER. I should advise it, sir.

(GILES *fetches his overcoat from the front hall, puts it on and returns to the window.* TROTTER *moves* C *below the refectory table and writes in his notebook*)

Take my torch, sir. It's behind the curtain.

(GILES *climbs out through the window and exits.* TROTTER *crosses to the library door up* L *and exits. After a short pause he re-enters, switches off the library light, goes up to the window, shuts it and closes the curtain. He crosses to the fire and sinks into the large armchair. After a pause he rises and goes to the door down L)*

(*Calling*) Mrs Ralston, count twenty and then begin to play.

(TROTTER *shuts the door down L, moves to the stairs and looks off. "Three Blind Mice" is heard being played on the piano. After a pause, he moves down R and switches off the R wall brackets, then moves up R and switches off the L wall brackets. He moves quickly down to the table lamp and switches it on, then crosses down L to the door)*

(*Calling*) Mrs Ralston! Mrs Ralston!

(MOLLIE *enters down L and moves below the sofa)*

MOLLIE. Yes, what is it?

(TROTTER *shuts the door down L and leans against the downstage side of the door reveal)*

You're looking very pleased with yourself. Have you got what you wanted?

TROTTER. I've got exactly what I wanted.

MOLLIE. You know who the murderer is?

TROTTER. Yes, I know.

MOLLIE. Which of them?

TROTTER. *You* ought to know, Mrs Ralston.

MOLLIE. I?

TROTTER. Yes, you've been extraordinarily foolish, you know. You've run a very good chance of being killed by holding out on me. As a result, you've been in serious danger more than once.

MOLLIE. I don't know what you mean.

TROTTER (*moving slowly above the sofa table to R of the sofa; still quite natural and friendly*) Come now, Mrs Ralston. We policemen aren't quite so dumb as you think. All along I've realized that you had first-hand knowledge of the Longridge Farm affair. You knew Mrs Boyle was the magistrate concerned. In fact, you knew all about it. Why didn't you speak up and say so?

MOLLIE (*very much affected*) I don't understand. I wanted to forget—forget. (*She sits at the L end of the sofa*)

TROTTER. Your maiden name was Waring?

MOLLIE. Yes.

TROTTER. Miss Waring. You taught school—in the school where those children went.

MOLLIE. Yes.

TROTTER. It's true, isn't it, that Jimmy, the child who died, managed to get a letter posted to you? (*He sits at the R end of the sofa*) The letter begged for help—help from his kind young teacher. You never answered that letter.

MOLLIE. I couldn't. I never got it.

E

TROTTER. You just—didn't bother.

MOLLIE. That's not true. I was ill. I went down with pneumonia that very day. The letter was put aside with others. It was weeks afterwards that I found it with a lot of other letters. And by then that poor child was dead . . . (*Her eyes close*) Dead—dead . . . Waiting for me to do something—hoping—gradually losing hope . . . Oh, it's haunted me ever since . . . If only I hadn't been ill—if only I'd known . . . Oh, it's monstrous that such things should happen.

TROTTER (*his voice suddenly thick*) Yes, it's monstrous. (*He takes a revolver out of his pocket*)

MOLLIE. I thought the police didn't carry revolvers . . . (*She suddenly sees* TROTTER'S *face, and gasps in horror*)

TROTTER. The police don't . . . I'm not a policeman, Mrs Ralston. You thought I was a policeman because I rang up from a call box and said I was speaking from police headquarters and that Sergeant Trotter was on his way. I cut the telephone wires before I came to the front door. You know who I am, Mrs Ralston? I'm Georgie—I'm Jimmy's brother, Georgie.

MOLLIE. Oh. (*She looks round her wildly*)

TROTTER (*rising*) You'd better not scream, Mrs Ralston—because if you do I shall fire this revolver . . . I'd like to talk to you a little. (*He turns away*) I said I'd like to talk to you a little. Jimmy died. (*His manner becomes very simple and childlike*) That nasty cruel woman killed him. They put her in prison. Prison wasn't bad enough for her. I said I'd kill her one day . . . I did, too. In the fog. It was great fun. I hope Jimmy knows. "I'll kill them all when I've grown up." That's what I said to myself. Because grown-ups can do anything they like. (*Gaily*) I'm going to kill you in a minute.

MOLLIE. You'd better not. (*She tries very hard to be persuasive*) You'll never get safely away, you know.

TROTTER (*pettishly*) Someone's hidden my skis! I can't find them. But it doesn't matter. I don't really mind if I get away or not. I'm tired. It's all been such fun. Watching you all. And pretending to be a policeman.

MOLLIE. That revolver will make a lot of noise.

TROTTER. It will rather. Much better to do it the usual way, and take you by the neck. (*He slowly approaches her, whistling* "*Three Blind Mice*") The last little mouse in the trap. (*He drops the revolver on the sofa, and leans over her with his left hand on her mouth and his right hand on her neck*)

(MISS CASEWELL *and* MAJOR METCALF *appear in the arch up* R)

MISS CASEWELL. Georgie, Georgie, you know me, don't you? Don't you remember the farm, Georgie? The animals, that fat old pig, and the day the bull chased us across the field. And the dogs. (*She crosses to* L *of the sofa table*)

Trotter. Dogs?

Miss Casewell. Yes, Spot and Plain.

Trotter. Kathy?

Miss Casewell. Yes, Kathy—you remember me now, don't you?

Trotter. Kathy, it is you. What are you doing here? (*He rises and moves to* R *of the sofa table*)

Miss Casewell. I came to England to find you. I didn't recognize you until you twirled your hair the way you always used to do.

(Trotter *twirls his hair*)

Yes, you always did it. Georgie, come with me. (*Firmly*) You're coming with me.

Trotter. Where are we going?

Miss Casewell (*gently, as if to a child*) It's all right, Georgie. I'm taking you somewhere where they will look after you, and see that you won't do any more harm.

(Miss Casewell *exits up the stairs, leading* Trotter *by the hand.* Major Metcalf *switches on the lights, crosses to the stairs, and looks up*)

Major Metcalf (*calling*) Ralston! Ralston!

(Major Metcalf *exits up the stairs.*
      Giles *enters from the arch up* R. *He rushes over to Mollie on the sofa, sits and takes her in his arms, placing the revolver on the sofa table*)

Giles. Mollie, Mollie, are you all right? Darling, darling.

Mollie. Oh, Giles.

Giles. Whoever would have dreamt it was Trotter?

Mollie. He's mad, quite mad.

Giles. Yes, but you . . .

Mollie. I was mixed up in it all, I taught in the school. It wasn't my fault—but he thought I could have saved that child.

Giles. You should have told me.

Mollie. I wanted to forget.

(Major Metcalf *enters from the stairs and comes to* c)

Major Metcalf. Everything's under control. He will be unconscious soon with a sedative—his sister's looking after him. Poor fellow's as mad as a hatter, of course. I've had my suspicions of him all along.

Mollie. You did? Didn't you believe he was a policeman?

Major Metcalf. I knew he wasn't a policeman. You see, Mrs Ralston, I'm a policeman.

Mollie. You?

Major Metcalf. As soon as we got hold of that notebook

with "Monkswell Manor" written in it, we saw it was vital to have someone on the spot. When it was put to him, Major Metcalf agreed to let me take his place. I couldn't understand it when Trotter turned up. (*He sees the revolver on the sofa table and picks it up*)

MOLLIE. And Casewell is his sister?

MAJOR METCALF. Yes, it seems she recognized him just before this last business. Didn't know what to do, but fortunately came to me about it, just in time. Well, it's started to thaw, help should be here pretty soon. (*Moving up to the arch* R) Oh, by the way, Mrs Ralston, I'll remove those skis. I hid them on top of the four-poster.

(MAJOR METCALF *exits up* R)

MOLLIE. And I thought it was Paravicini.

GILES. I gather they'll examine that car of his rather carefully. I shouldn't be surprised if they found a thousand or so Swiss watches in the spare wheel. Yes, that's his line of business, nasty little bit of goods. Mollie, I believe you thought I was . . .

MOLLIE. Giles, what were you doing in London yesterday?

GILES. Darling, I was buying you an anniversary present. We've been married just a year today.

MOLLIE. Oh. That's what I went to London for, and I didn't want you to know.

GILES. No.

(MOLLIE *rises, goes to the desk cupboard, and takes out the parcel.* GILES *rises and goes to* R *of the sofa table*)

MOLLIE (*handing him the parcel*) They're cigars. I do hope they're all right.

GILES (*unwrapping the parcel*) Oh, darling, how sweet of you. They're splendid.

MOLLIE. You will smoke them?

GILES (*heroically*) I'll smoke them.

MOLLIE. What's my present?

GILES. Oh yes, I forgot all about your present. (*He rushes up to the chest in the entrance hall, takes out the hat-box and returns. Proudly*) It's a hat.

MOLLIE (*taken aback*) A hat? But I practically never wear one.

GILES. Just for best.

MOLLIE (*lifting out the hat*) Oh, how lovely, darling.

GILES. Put it on.

MOLLIE. Later, when my hair's done properly.

GILES. It is all right, isn't it? The girl in the shop said it was the last thing in hats.

(MOLLIE *puts the hat on.* GILES *moves below the desk.* MAJOR METCALF *rushes in up* R)

Major Metcalf. Mrs Ralston! Mrs Ralston! There's a terrible smell of burning coming from the kitchen.

(Mollie *rushes up* R *towards the kitchen*)

Mollie (*wailing*)   Oh, my pie!

QUICK CURTAIN

FURNITURE AND PROPERTY PLOT

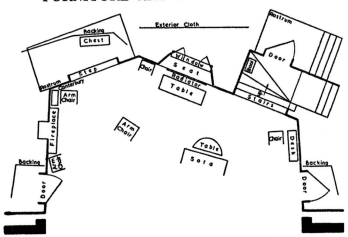

On stage—Refectory table. *On it:* magazines, newspapers
    Sofa. *On it:* 2 cushions
    Sofa table. *On it:* table lamp, ashtray, table lighter, cigarette box
          with cigarettes, magazine, vase of flowers (winter)
    Desk. *On it:* telephone, telephone pad, pencils, radio, ashtray, small
         mirror
        On first shelf: letters, file of letters, blotter, ABC railway guide,
          phone directories
        On other shelves: books
    2 chairs
    Large armchair (R)
    Armchair (C). *On it:* cushion
    Canterbury. *In it:* magazines, newspapers
    Small Victorian armchair
    In fireplace: grate, fire-irons
    On mantelpiece: clock, 2 mugs (1 with spills), china coffee-pot, ash-
      tray, cigarette box
    In entrance hall: oak chest
            Off stage: batten with 6 coat-hooks
    On staircase L: small oak stool
    By window seat: radiator

ACT I

SCENE 1

Set—*On stage: On desk:* list of rooms
        On staircase L: " Monkwell Manor" sign board

    Off stage R: Cigars in box wrapped in brown paper (MOLLIE)
             Hat-box with hat, wrapped (GILES)
             Suitcase (CHRISTOPHER)
             Suitcase, magazines, gloves (MRS BOYLE)

Suitcase (MAJOR METCALF)
Suitcase, newspaper, handbag (MISS CASEWELL)
Small black hold-all bag (PARAVICINI)

Personal—MOLLIE: gloves with bus ticket, handbag, watch

Curtains open
Doors closed

ACT I
SCENE 2

Strike—Paravicini's bag
     Newspaper

Check—In armchair C: glove with ticket

Set—On sofa: book
    In small armchair down R: book
    In large armchair: writing case
    By fireplace: 2 logs
    On mantelpiece: lighter

Off stage R—Duster and vacuum cleaner (MOLLIE)
          Torch, skis (TROTTER)
          Logs in cardboard box (GILES)

Off stage up L—Ski sticks (TROTTER)

Personal—MAJOR METCALF: pipe, tobacco pouch, matches
         MISS CASEWELL: cigarettes in packet, lighter
         TROTTER: notebook and pencil

Curtains open

ACT II

Strike—Duster
     Logs and box
     Books

Check—Radio switch off

Set—On sofa: Miss Casewell's handbag with letter
    On window seat: torch
    On refectory table: sheet of notepaper
    In entrance hall: Giles' overcoat with *Evening News* in pocket

Off stage R—Revolver (TROTTER)

Personal—PARAVICINI: cigars in case, piercer, matches
         MAJOR METCALF: pipe, tobacco pouch, matches
         TROTTER: notebook, pencil

Curtains closed

LIGHTING PLOT

Property fittings required:
5 wall brackets, table lamp (all practical); fire

ACT I   SCENE 1

A lounge hall
Interior. Late afternoon; winter

The Apparent Sources of Light are first from the window and later from the brackets over the fireplace and the table lamp (LC)

The Main Acting Areas are round the sofa (LC), by the fireplace (R), at the refectory table (up C), round the armchair (C) and by the arches up R and L

Off Stage Lighting: cold, grey, (snow) outside window; strips outside doors and outside arch up R (each with a practical switch); red glow from fire

To open: Complete BLACK-OUT

Cue   1   VOICE ON RADIO: "and according to Scotland Yard . . ."   (page 1)
      Creep in stage lights (for winter afternoon) slowly

Cue   2   MOLLIE enters and turns on wall brackets R   (page 2)
      Bring in wall brackets (R) and lighting round fireplace and armchairs

Cue   3   MOLLIE switches on table lamp   (page 3)
      Bring in table lamp and lighting round sofa and desk (L)

ACT I   SCENE 2

The same
Afternoon

To open: Brackets and table lamp off. Strips on. Fire on.

Cue   1   MAJOR METCALF: "think he's escaped from a lunatic asylum . . ."
                                                    (page 16)
      The lights fade gradually until the stage is dimly lit

Cue   2   MOLLIE switches on wall brackets R   (page 30)
      Bring in full lighting

Cue   2a   GILES finds bus ticket in glove   (page 32)
      If desired, the lights may gradually fade until the next cue

Cue   3   A hand clicks off the switch down R   (page 33)
      BLACK-OUT

Cue   4   MOLLIE enters and switches on the lights
      Bring in 2 wall brackets (L) and one in entrance hall, and all lighting.

ACT II

The same
Ten minutes later

To open: All brackets on. Strips on. Fire on.

Cue   1   TROTTER switches off wall brackets R   (page 61)
      Take out wall brackets (R) and lighting round fireplace

Cue   2   TROTTER switches off rest of wall brackets   (page 61)
      Take out remaining wall brackets and lighting round sofa and desk

Cue   3   TROTTER switches on table (LC)   (page 61)
      Bring in a circle of light round sofa only

Cue   4   MAJOR METCALF switches on lights   (page 63)
      Bring in opening lighting

MUSIC AND SOUND PLOT

Required: Special recordings of:
    Three Blind Mice (Orchestral)
    Three Blind Mice (Piano)
    BBC News
    Mechanics of Fear

    Recordings of:

Flight of the Bumble Bee	Parlophone No. R2848
Trumpet Blues	Parlophone No. R2852
Four Sea Interludes	Decca No. AK1704

ACT I

SCENE 1

Cue	1	Before the CURTAIN rises *Fade in orchestral music of "Three Blind Mice"*	(page 1)
Cue	2	After rise of CURTAIN *Fade out orchestral music*	(page 1)
Cue	3	After police whistles *Fade in BBC news announcement*	(page 1)
Cue	4	MOLLIE switches off radio *Cut BBC news announcement*	(page 2)
Cue	5	MOLLIE switches on radio *Fade in BBC news announcement*	(page 4)
Cue	6	MOLLIE switches off radio *Cut BBC news announcement*	(page 5)

ACT I

SCENE 2

Cue	1	MISS CASEWELL switches on radio *Fade in "Flight of the Bumble Bee" (halfway through)*	(page 17)
Cue	2	CHRISTOPHER turns down volume *Reduce volume*	(page 18)
Cue	3	At end of record *Mix to "Trumpet Blues"*	
Cue	4	CHRISTOPHER turns up volume *Increase volume to very loud*	(page 18)
Cue	5	MOLLIE, at telephone, switches off *Cut record*	(page 19)
Cue	6	After MRS BOYLE's exit *Start record of piano "Three Blind Mice" and play to end*	(page 30)
Cue	7	TROTTER's re-entry *Start record of piano "Three Blind Mice"*	(page 31)
Cue	8	TROTTER opens door of drawing-room *Swell volume*	(page 31)
Cue	9	TROTTER closes door *Decrease volume to previous mark*	(page 31)

Cue 10   Mrs Boyle switches on radio   (page 33)
           Fade in "Sea Interlude No. 4" loud

Cue 11   Mrs Boyle re-tunes radio   (page 33)
           Mix to "Mechanics of Fear"

Cue 12   Mrs Boyle re-tunes radio for music   (page 33)
           Fade out "Mechanics of Fear" and fade in Sea Interlude
           No. 4 loud, continuing to fall of Curtain

ACT II

Cue 1   Trotter calls Mollie   (page 61)
           Start record of piano "Three Blind Mice" and play to end

THE OFFICE PLAYS
Two full length plays by Adam Bock

THE RECEPTIONIST
Comedy / 2m., 2f. Interior
At the start of a typical day in the Northeast Office, Beverly deals effortlessly with ringing phones and her colleague's romantic troubles. But the appearance of a charming rep from the Central Office disrupts the friendly routine. And as the true nature of the company's business becomes apparent, The Receptionist raises disquieting, provocative questions about the consequences of complicity with evil.

"...Mr. Bock's poisoned Post-it note of a play."
- New York Times

"Bock's intense initial focus on the routine goes to the heart of
The Receptionist's pointed, painfully timely allegory... elliptical,
provocative play..."
- Time Out New York

THE THUGS
Comedy / 2m, 6f / Interior
The Obie Award winning dark comedy about work, thunder and the mysterious things that are happening on the 9th floor of a big law firm. When a group of temps try to discover the secrets that lurk in the hidden crevices of their workplace, they realize they would rather believe in gossip and rumors than face dangerous realities.

"Bock starts you off giggling, but leaves you with a chill."
- Time Out New York

"... a delightfully paranoid little nightmare that is both more
chillingly realistic and pointedly absurd than anything
John Grisham ever dreamed up."
- New York Times

NO SEX PLEASE, WE'RE BRITISH
Anthony Marriott and Alistair Foot

Farce / 7 m., 3 f. / Int.

A young bride who lives above a bank with her husband who is the assistant manager, innocently sends a mail order off for some Scandinavian glassware. What comes is Scandinavian pornography. The plot revolves around what is to be done with the veritable floods of pornography, photographs, books, films and eventually girls that threaten to engulf this happy couple. The matter is considerably complicated by the man's mother, his boss, a visiting bank inspector, a police superintendent and a muddled friend who does everything wrong in his reluctant efforts to set everything right, all of which works up to a hilarious ending of closed or slamming doors. This farce ran in London over eight years and also delighted Broadway audiences.

"Titillating and topical."
- "NBC TV"

"A really funny Broadway show."
- "ABC TV"

DANGER- GIRLS WORKING
James Reach

Mystery Comedy / 11f / Unit Set

At a New York girl's boarding house, there is a newspaper woman who wants to write a novel, a wise cracking shop girl, the serious music student, a faded actress, a girl looking for romance, the kid who wants to crash Broadway and other boarders. The landlady, is the proud custodian of the "McCarthy Collection," a group of perfect uncut diamonds. When it disappears from the safe, the newspaper woman is given two hours to solve the case before the police are called. Suspicion is cleverly shifted from one to the other of the girls and there's a very surprising solution.

THE CEMETERY CLUB
Ivan Menchell

Comedy / 1m, 5f / Multiple Sets

Three Jewish widows meet once a month for tea before going to visit their husband's graves. Ida is sweet tempered and ready to begin a new life, Lucille is a feisty embodiment of the girl who just wants to have fun, and Doris is priggish and judgmental, particularly when Sam the butcher enters the scene. He meets the widows while visiting his wife's grave. Doris and Lucille squash the budding romance between Sam and Ida. They are guilt stricken when this nearly breaks Ida's heart. The Broadway production starred Eileen Heckart as Lucille.

"Funny, sweet tempered, moving."
– *Boston Globe*

"Very touching and humorous. An evening of pure pleasure that will make you glad you went to the theatre."
– *Washington Journal Newspapers*

OTHER TITLES AVAILABLE FROM SAMUEL FRENCH

SAME TIME, NEXT YEAR
Bernard Slade

Comedy / 1m, 1f / Interior

One of the most popular romantic comedies of the century, *Same Time, Next Year* ran four years on Broadway, winning a Tony Award for lead actress Ellen Burstyn, who later recreated her role in the successful motion picture. It remains one of the world's most widely produced plays. The plot follows a love affair between two people, Doris and George, married to others, who rendezvous once a year. Twenty-five years of manners and morals are hilariously and touchingly played out by the lovers.

"Delicious wit, compassion, a sense of humor and a feel for nostalgia."
– *The New York Times*

"Genuinely funny and genuinely romantic."
– *The New York Post*

OTHER TITLES AVAILABLE FROM SAMUEL FRENCH

ENTER A FREE MAN
Tom Stoppard

Comedy / 5m, 3f / Combined Interior

Riley's a dreamer with all sorts of off-beat inventions, and his latest one is a double gummed envelope that can be used twice: once for sending and then turned inside out for replying. At home Riley is not well liked. His daughter is going to run away and marry a motorcyclist who turns out to be already married, and she can no longer support her dad in his unemployed habits. But this matters little to Riley, for he has this envelope deal, and also an indoor watering device for flowers. Trouble is, all his devices fall through including the indoor watering device when it is discovered you can't turn it off. And his dreams continue to burst in his face.

"A splendid full fledged comic creation."
– *London Observer*